The Art of Public Speaking: Lessons from the Greatest Speeches in History

John R. Hale, Ph.D.

PUBLISHED BY:

THE GREAT COURSES
Corporate Headquarters
4840 Westfields Boulevard, Suite 500
Chantilly, Virginia 20151-2299
Phone: 1-800-832-2412
Fax: 703-378-3819
www.thegreatcourses.com

Printed in the United States of America

John R. Hale, Ph.D.

Director of Liberal Studies
University of Louisville

Professor John R. Hale, Director of Liberal Studies at the University of Louisville, is an archaeologist with fieldwork experience in England, Scandinavia, Portugal, Greece, Turkey, and the Ohio River Valley. At the University of Louisville, Professor Hale teaches introductory courses on archaeology and specialized courses on the Bronze Age, the ancient Greeks, the Roman world, Celtic cultures, Vikings, and nautical and underwater archaeology.

Archaeology has been the focus of Professor Hale's career, from his undergraduate studies at Yale University to his research at the University of Cambridge, where he received his Ph.D. The subject of his dissertation was the Bronze Age ancestry of the Viking longship, a study that involved field surveys of ship designs in prehistoric rock art in southern Norway and Sweden. During more than 30 years of archaeological work, Professor Hale has excavated at a Romano-British town in Lincolnshire, England, as well as at a Roman villa in Portugal; has carried out interdisciplinary studies of ancient oracle sites in Greece and Turkey, including the famed Delphic oracle; and has participated in an undersea search in Greek waters for lost fleets from the Greek and Persian wars. In addition, Professor Hale is a member of a scientific team developing and refining a method for dating mortar, concrete, and plaster from ancient buildings—a method that employs radiocarbon analysis with an accelerator mass spectrometer.

Professor Hale published *Lords of the Sea: The Epic Story of the Athenian Navy and the Birth of Democracy* in 2009. In addition, he has published his work in *Antiquity*, *Journal of Roman Archaeology*, *The Classical Bulletin*, and *Scientific American*. Most of Professor Hale's work is interdisciplinary and involves collaborations with geologists, chemists, nuclear physicists, historians, zoologists, botanists, physical anthropologists, geographers, and art historians.

Professor Hale has deep experience as a public speaker, having given thousands of talks in his career. He has received numerous awards for his distinguished teaching, including the Panhellenic Teacher of the Year Award and the Delphi Center Award. He has toured the United States and Canada as a lecturer for the Archaeological Institute of America and has presented lecture series at museums and universities in Finland, South Africa, Australia, and New Zealand.

Professor Hale is the instructor of three other Great Courses: *Exploring the Roots of Religion*, *The Greek and Persian Wars*, and *Classical Archaeology of Ancient Greece and Rome*. ■

Table of Contents

INTRODUCTION

Professor Biography i
Course Scope 1

LECTURE GUIDES

LECTURE 1
Overcome Obstacles—Demosthenes of Athens 2

LECTURE 2
Practice Your Delivery—Patrick Henry 16

LECTURE 3
Be Yourself—Elizabeth I to Her Army 30

LECTURE 4
Find Your Humorous Voice—Will Rogers 44

LECTURE 5
Make It a Story—Marie Curie on Discovery 59

LECTURE 6
Use the Power of Three—Paul to His People 74

LECTURE 7
Build a Logical Case—Susan B. Anthony 88

LECTURE 8
Paint Pictures in Words—Tecumseh on Unity 104

LECTURE 9
Focus on Your Audience—Gandhi on Trial 118

LECTURE 10
Share a Vision—Martin Luther King's Dream 133

Table of Contents

LECTURE 11
Change Minds and Hearts—Mark Antony 149

LECTURE 12
Call for Positive Action—Lincoln at Gettysburg 164

SUPPLEMENTAL MATERIAL

Bibliography 179
Credits 180

The Art of Public Speaking: Lessons from the Greatest Speeches in History

Scope:

How should one go about learning how to write and present a speech, no matter the occasion? Why not study lessons from history's greatest speeches and speakers? This unique course explores the greatest speeches in history and sets out practical tips that we can use for any public speaking situation. Our historic speechmakers include Demosthenes, Saint Paul, Queen Elizabeth, Patrick Henry, Tecumseh, and Abraham Lincoln. The lectures use historical case studies to glean insight into every aspect of public speaking, from topic and style to opening and closing. The power of a call to action: Abraham Lincoln's oration at Gettysburg. The power of presentation: 55-year-old Queen Elizabeth delivering a stirring call to arms in the field—"to live or die amongst you all"—among soldiers on the eve of battle with the Spanish Armada. The power of sharing a vision: Martin Luther King Jr.'s "I Have a Dream" speech. We unlock the secrets of history's greatest speeches in a course that is as practical as it is fascinating.

Each of the 12 lectures offers take-away points that are illustrated with a presentation of the featured speech, including background on the speaker and the context of the speech. Additional insights are provided by references to many other historic speakers. We will consider how their lessons apply to everyday modern situations—eulogies, reports, political addresses, legal arguments, business proposals, toasts, conferences, pregame speeches, sermons, classroom lectures, and "how-to" explanations—in which you may find yourself called upon to speak in public. ■

Overcome Obstacles—Demosthenes of Athens

Lecture 1

Rhetoric is as noble an art as exists on this planet; rhetoric is the art of clothing in words and in gestures and in presentation to a group the ideas that you have in the most effective way possible.

Winston Churchill once said, "There is nothing like oratory," and to paraphrase him, he said, "It is a skill that can turn a commoner into a king." I believe that's true; I believe that public speaking is a skill that everyone should try to acquire. We're going to have 12 guest lecturers in the course of our time together: I want to share this podium with the likes of Demosthenes of Athens, Queen Elizabeth I of England, Martin Luther King Jr., Mahatma Gandhi, Abraham Lincoln, and many others. They will each be featured in a speech or set of speeches that made a difference to the world and to them, but more important, speeches that make a point about public speaking. I hope that you will end this course with a greater understanding of what makes good public speaking, a greater appreciation of what an important part of your life public speaking can become, and greater incentive to tackle the challenge of getting over your obstacles and starting to speak in public yourself.

The genius of rhetoric that I would like to have lead us into this world of speechmaking is Demosthenes of Athens, who lived in the 5th century B.C. Demosthenes was a genius who, at a time when Athens's fortunes were sinking, tried to revive his city's power through his own speeches. But nobody would have guessed from looking at him as a boy that it could have happened. Demosthenes was born to a rich family, but his father died when he was very small. He was brought up by the womenfolk in the family, outside the public sphere. He did not go to the gymnasium with the other boys; he did not toughen himself up. He grew up alone with books. One of his books was *The History of the Peloponnesian War* by Thucydides, another Athenian. Demosthenes had a copy that he read eight times; he memorized lots of it, and what he was memorizing in many cases were speeches.

Demosthenes's first step was to try to become a good speaker by opening up scrolls, reading somebody else's speech, and committing it to memory; because in Athens, if you were speaking in a law court of the public Assembly, you had to speak from memory. Demosthenes soon learned that he had some serious problems to overcome: Physically, he was weak; he walked around stooped-shouldered with a frown all the time. He had a speech impediment; we don't know exactly what, but it may have been a lisp. People laughed at him when he spoke as a boy, and he knew he was going to have to get over that if he intended to have a career as a public speaker as a man.

When Demosthenes turned 18, he discovered that his guardians had embezzled all of his inheritance from his father. The only way that he would be able to get it back was to go to court, where he would have to speak for himself. So he went down to the seashore where he could be completely alone and began a course of self-improvement to make him a man that people would listen to in a court of law. He used a little prop, a little aid, that he invented himself as a method for improving elocution: a pebble. To get over his speech impediment, he would put a pebble in his mouth, and he would then speak, working to get his tongue and to get his palate and to get his lips around that pebble so that he could be understood even with that stone in his mouth. He would take those speeches by Thucydides and others and train his own speaking apparatus—tongue, palate, lips—so that even with the pebble, he could still be clearly understood. In this way, Demosthenes overcame the first of his obstacles: the speech impediment.

In polite conversation, it's supposed to be a bad thing to talk about yourself; in public speaking, most of the time it's essential.

Second, he was aware of his weakness of breath. He began to run up hills, declaiming speeches that he'd memorized until he got to the point that his wind was so good, he could run and speak the speech and not sound out of breath. Finally, he practiced speaking at the seashore, trying to outshout the waves themselves so that when he got up in front of that jury of 501 people or in front of the entire Assembly of Athens, everybody would be able to hear him. There has never been such a concentrated attack on the art of rhetoric as young Demosthenes undertook while still a teenager. He went to the court and won his case. Then his vision grew wider: He wanted to speak in public; he wanted to share the idealism that he had acquired from reading Thucydides's history about the glorious days of Athens in his own time of decadence and decay.

By this time, Demosthenes had become a sea captain, in charge of a warship. This had a powerful effect on his credibility; he could speak from personal knowledge. I urge you to do that in every speech you make. If you're toasting a wedding couple, talk about your personal knowledge of them; if you're lecturing on a subject, talk about your own experiences with that subject. In polite conversation it's supposed to be a bad thing to talk about yourself; in public speaking, most of the time it's essential.

Demosthenes used his new experience as a sea captain in crafting metaphors and images, painting pictures with words. People remembered his words until their dying day; and that's another thing for you to consider as you plan your public speeches, be they short or long: Someone out there may find in what you say the words that crystallize a feeling, an event, a moment and remember them as the words of Demosthenes were remembered by his fellow countrymen. ■

Take-Away Points

1. Make up your mind that you can and will overcome fears and obstacles.

2. Practice, practice, practice every aspect of public speaking.

3. Use cross-training in acting, sports, and other fields to improve your skills.

4. Work on memorization.

5. Accept early failures, and persist with your efforts.

Overcome Obstacles—Demosthenes of Athens

Lecture 1—Transcript

Hello, and welcome to your course on "The Art of Public Speaking." My name is John Hale. I'm an archaeologist at the University of Louisville in Kentucky, and it's going to be my pleasure to spend 12 lectures with you in talking about what I think is the most neglected skill in the entire repertoire of things you can learn in the world today. Winston Churchill once said, "There is nothing like oratory," and to paraphrase him, he said, "It is a skill that can turn a commoner into a king." I believe that's true; I believe that public speaking is something that everyone should try to acquire; if you are a citizen in a democracy, you need to be able to speak in public. But also, if you're a member of a family, you will be attending weddings and be expected to give a toast to the bride and the groom; or a funeral, and a eulogy for a dead loved one; or just a congratulatory speech at someone's birthday. All of these call for public speaking skills. In our ordinary life, there are times when you want to address a book group about a book that you've read or talk to a neighborhood association about something important to you; there are times when you need to stand up in a courtroom or for a planning commission and make a case; and there are other times when you are simply trying to share your own skills, your own background, to someone who might be able to give you a job. Certain professions call for public speaking: lawyers, doctors, people in the military, clergy; all kinds of salespeople, businesspeople who either need to sell themselves or a product or an idea; all of these are folks who are going to need to be effective public speakers, and that means just about everyone.

This skill is often devalued. Lots of people think that public speaking is something that you shouldn't think about; that it's rhetoric or mere oratory. These are considered pejorative terms; rhetoric is supposed to be fancy verbal flourishes that hide meaning rather than convey it. It's nothing of the sort; rhetoric is as noble an art as exists on this planet; rhetoric is the art of clothing in words and in gestures and in presentation to a group the ideas that you have in the most effective way possible. That's what rhetoric is, that's what oratory is all about; that's the skill we're going after in this course.

The fact that you are here means that you are concerned about your skills as someone who can speak in public; it means that you have decided to take some steps, and that's the most important thing at all. We're going to have 12 guest lecturers in the course of our time together: I want to share this podium with the likes of Demosthenes of Athens, Queen Elizabeth I of England, Martin Luther King, Jr., Mahatma Gandhi, Abraham Lincoln, and many others. They will each be featured in a speech or set of speeches that made a difference to the world and to them, but more important, in my view, speeches that make a point; speeches that help you understand more clearly, with a vivid example, something about public speaking. At the same time, I—as the presiding professor who ties these 12 guests together—am going to try be modeling what I think is good public speaking to you all the time.

What is my qualification to even be up here in front of this camera? I'm a teacher; and that means that early on in my life I decided it was my mission in my case to speak for the past, a past that cannot speak for itself. There are other missions, there are other people, but that's my mission. Early on, I got over stage fright in a way that we're going to be talking about in a little bit, and I found that I was able to stand up in front of a group and present an explanation of archaeology that I had done or that I had read about others carrying out; trying to explain ancient monuments, ancient cultures, vanished civilizations. This had become my world; I wanted other people to understand it as their world. I was lucky to go to an elementary school that helped me become an effective public speaker very early in my life, to the point where now I think I've probably given—I did add it up when I was preparing for these lectures—about 2,000 public speaking presentations, most of them as lectures, as a teacher trying to explain, trying to inform; that's one of the goals of public speaking: to teach, along with to persuade, to congratulate, to praise, to challenge, and many others. But mine was mainly about teaching.

This school that I went to, this public school, from third grade on—I should give it credit: Green Valley Grade School, New Albany, Indiana—had a tradition: Every class had to write, produce, and act a play, and every student had to have a speaking part. The result was we all got over stage fright, because everybody was in it together; we all had to be up there on the stage in the gymnasium, and I can remember the teachers in a row at the back of the gym shouting to us, "Louder," "Clearer," "Slower," "I can't understand you," "You're talking to the front row, you need to be talking to the back row." By the time I graduated from Green Valley Grade School in sixth grade, I, like the rest of my class, had become a person who felt comfortable on a stage, felt comfortable talking. I think it's a great sin that this kind of training isn't given in every school; but if you are signed up for this course, it may be a skill that was somehow neglected in your early years.

I'd like to try to share some of the ideas on how to get to this point of calmness and certitude with you. I hope that by hearing from my own experience, by sharing with you—perhaps more to the point—the experiences and the words of these giants among public speakers, these historical greats, and finally by extracting from their words three to six lessons in each of our lectures you will end this course with a greater understanding of what makes good public speaking, of a greater appreciation of what an important part of your life public speaking can become, and finally a feeling of much greater incentive to tackle the challenge of getting over your obstacles, getting over your fears, and starting to speak in public yourself. All of this is wrapped up in this world of rhetoric. You may also have heard of some special rhetoric terms that are used for forms of speech, modes of address; I'm less concerned with those. I'm more concerned with you; I'm more concerned with the kinds of situations you are likely to face as a public speaker.

The first thing we have to do is get over stage fright. There are other obstacles, too; our featured speaker today, Demosthenes of Athens, had a formidable array of obstacles between him as a young man who'd grown up way out of the world and out of public life, who was determined to turn himself into a speaker, but the first thing he had to manage was fear. I want to read you an extract from a speech by Mark Twain that he composed in honor of his daughter, who was a contralto singer. In the early 1900s she gave a recital and he gave a little speech after she finished singing; and he harked back to his own experience to what we call "performance anxiety." "Public speaking anxiety" (PSA) is just a branch of performance anxiety where the palms start to sweat, the breath seems short, the legs begin to shake, your mind goes blank; all of these things happen with performance anxiety. This is Mark Twain's expression and memory of his first speech:

My heart goes out in sympathy to anyone who is making his first appearance before an audience of human beings. …

I recall the occasion of my first appearance. San Francisco knew me then only as a reporter, and I was to make my bow to San Francisco as a lecturer. I knew that nothing short of compulsion would get me to the theater. So I bound myself by a hard-and-fast contract so that I could not escape. I got to the theater forty-five minutes before the hour set for the lecture. My knees were shaking so that I didn't know whether I could stand up. If there is an awful, horrible malady in the world, it is stage fright—and seasickness. They are a pair. …

It was dark and lonely behind the scenes in that theater, and I peeked through the little peek holes they have in theater curtains and looked into the big auditorium. That was dark and empty, too. By and by it lighted up, and the audience began to arrive. …

At last I began. I had the manuscript tucked under a United States flag in front of me where I could get at it in case of need. But I managed to get started without it. I walked up and down—I was young in those days and needed the exercise—and talked and talked. …

Well, after the first agonizing five minutes, my stage fright left me, never to return. I know if I was going to be hanged I could get up and make a good showing, and I intend to. But I shall never forget my feelings just before the agony left me.

Mark Twain was one of America's most popular public personalities. It's very hard to imagine that a Mark Twain would have ever suffered a moment's uncertainty, self-doubt, indecision when getting up in front of an audience, but we have his own word for it that he did; that he felt the same terror and shaking that all the rest of us have done.

I want you to notice the things that he did, the steps that he took in order to prepare himself for that speech: First of all, he made a compact with himself; he faced the fear, he faced the difficulties, and he said, "I shall go through with this, and I shall go to the theater 45 minutes early to be ready." This going to the theater 45 minutes early, that is very important; as we shall see in a later lecture, you always want to go and get to know your space. You want to see where you will be presenting; you want to try out your voice—although he does not specifically mention that—to hear it in the space so you know what it will be like when you begin to speak out and yours is the only voice suddenly there filling that auditorium. I don't know what was in his mind when he looked at those people, clearly many of them he already knew; in fact, in part of the speech I didn't give you, he talks about how he had actually planted some friends in the audience with instructions to laugh at his jokes and support his points. I don't know that it helped him, but I do know that getting there early, getting to know the space, visualizing the space with him in it talking was a critical step toward becoming master of the situation.

Then he tells us that he had his speech written out. This is an important thing to do early on in your career. You want to write down a speech, and you want to have it with you. If you choke up, if you get scared, if you feel like you can't go on or remember it, do what he was planning to do: Fish under that little American flag—that's a charming touch that there was that bit of bunting there for him to hide it under—and simply go back to your written speech. He was ready for the emergency. What was the result of all of this forethought, all of this preparation, all of that time being in the theater and speaking—if he was speaking before his own talk—and having the script ready? The result was when he came to the moment it took him just a short time to get over the wobbly knees, the catch in the throat, all of the things that make you feel you can't finish this speech; and by the end of the speech, he was the Mark Twain that America then came to know as the most popular public lecturer in the country. It became a major part of his career.

Mark Twain introduces us to the personal part of our course. I've divided these 12 lectures into three parts. The first part is about you: your experiences, your preparation, your character, your overcoming obstacles so that you become everything you can be as a public speaker. The second part is going to focus on the speech itself. We're going to be looking at examples of people who carefully crafted a message to the public and learn lessons from them about how to create that speech, the thing that Mark Twain had tucked under the American flag, that's the right speech for the right occasion. Finally, we're going to get you out there on that platform (in surrogate form) beside Abraham Lincoln, Martin Luther King, Marc Antony in Rome proclaiming over Julius Caesar's body, and others so that you get a sense of what it's like to face the audience, and above all to think about the audience. There's a silly thing that's said as a first piece of advice to many public speakers: Stand there and imagine your audience with no clothes on (or, in the G-rated version, in underwear). I think this is terrible advice. You want to come to respect your audience just as you respect yourself and as you respect your message. That's what this course is trying to do for you: get to that sense of respect for all concerned; that sense of capability.

The genius of rhetoric that I would like to have lead us into this world of speechmaking is Demosthenes of Athens. I spend a lot of time in fifth century B.C. Athens. It's the world I love best; I've written books about it; I study its naval affairs; and there is one genius, Demosthenes, who at a time when Athens's fortunes were sinking tried to revive his city's power through his own speeches. But nobody would have guessed from looking at him as a boy that it could have happened. Demosthenes was born to a rich family, but his father died when he was very small. He was brought up by the womenfolk in the family, which means he was brought up outside the public sphere. He did not go to the gymnasium with the other boys; he did not toughen himself up, get his lungs strong through running, get his body fit through wrestling, getting to know other boys and being part of society. He grew up alone with books. One of his books was *The History of the Peloponnesian War* by Thucydides, another Athenian and at that time a fairly recent publication. He had a copy that he read eight times; he memorized lots of it, and what he was memorizing in many cases were speeches.

Demosthenes's first step was to try to become a good speaker by opening up scrolls and reading somebody else's speech, and committing it to memory; because in Athens, if you were speaking in a law court of the public Assembly, you couldn't use Mark Twain's crutch of the little written out manuscript, you had to speak from memory. No one would respect you if you were reading from a scroll, as I've occasionally done now. The one time that he could read when he was up there was if he was reading someone else's testimony, or a piece of evidence in a law court, or a treaty if he were talking in a speech about policy, national diplomacy and negotiations with other countries. Just as you've seen me—and I'm trying to model and demonstrate works for you—picking out other people's words and reading them, he could sometimes do that. It was an effective break in the speech, it helped him focus, it helped the audience to focus; otherwise, he would be on his own. Demosthenes soon learned that he had some serious problems to overcome: His voice was weak, his chest was weak. Physically, he was a weakling; he walked around stooped-shouldered with a frown all the time. He had a speech impediment; we don't know exactly what it was, it may have been a lisp of some kind. At any rate, people laughed at him when he spoke as a boy, and he knew he was going to have to get over that if he intended to have a career as a public speaker as a man.

All of this happened as he was growing up; he probably didn't realize that it was going to really matter to him to be a public speaker until he turned 18, got a reckoning of his inheritance from his father, and discovered that his guardians had embezzled all of his money. The only way that he would be able to get his money back—the money that his father had left him—was to go to court, and in Athenian courts you had to speak for yourself. So he went down to the seashore where he could be completely alone, and began a course of self-improvement to make him a man that people would listen to in a court of law. He used a little prop, a little aid, that he invented himself as a method for improving elocution: He used a pebble. To get over that speech impediment, he would put a pebble in his mouth, and he would then speak, working to get his tongue and to get his palate and to get his lips around that pebble so that he could be understood even with that stone in his mouth. He would take those speeches by Thucydides and others and gradually trained his own speaking apparatus—tongue, palate, lips—so that even with the pebble, he could still be clearly understood. In this way, Demosthenes overcame the first of his obstacles: the speech impediment.

Second, he was aware of his weakness of breath. Near the seashore, there were hills. He began to run up those hills, declaiming speeches that he'd memorized until he got to the point that his wind was so good, he could run and speak the speech and not sound out of breath. Finally, he went down to the seashore and tried to be heard above the crashing of the surf on the shore; trying to outshout the waves themselves so that when he got up in front of that jury of 501 people or in front of the entire Assembly of Athens, everybody would be able to hear him. There has never been such a concentrated attack on the art of rhetoric as young Demosthenes undertook while he was still a teenager. That's the reason he's a hero to me; that's one of the reasons that I picked him to be the first of our 12 guest lecturers to lead you into this world of public speaking and the practice and practice and more practice that it takes to become competent in this field.

He went to the court and he won his case. Then his vision grew wider: He wanted to speak in public; he wanted to share the idealism that he had acquired from reading Thucydides's history about the glorious days of Athens in his own time of decadence and decay. He began to prepare a speech to deliver himself to the Assembly. It was about reforming the navy. He got up—he wasn't known to have had a great deal of experience—and his speech was very technical. There was nothing about his own opinions or life or feelings in it—it could have been written by anybody—and it made no impression at all. This, I think, is another lesson we need to take from Demosthenes: Don't expect to succeed the very first time; don't expect that your first speech will have them with Mark Twain rolling in the aisles, or with Demosthenes up there—he had hoped for a great show of approval from the Athenian Assembly—don't expect that; and don't beat up on yourself if you do fail the first time, if you fall short. You are probably your own toughest critic. Please remember, your audience wants you to succeed. They will have picked out whatever was good in your speech for you, and you just need to go on. Learn from the mistakes, learn from what seemed week or ineffective.

He learned: Within a year of his first speech, he was back on the podium. He had found an antagonist of Athens: Philip of Macedon, a king, the father of Alexander the Great, who threatened Athenian freedom. Demosthenes, this scrawny youngster, decided to point the finger at Philip, show the world how he was gradually trying to take over the liberty of Greece and make it all one big Macedonian realm. By this time, he had become a sea captain himself, in charge of a warship. This had a powerful effect on his credibility; he could speak from personal knowledge. I urge you to do that in every speech you make. If you're toasting a wedding couple, talk about your personal knowledge of them; if you're lecturing on a subject, talk about your own experiences with that subject. Please do not think that nobody wants to hear about you. In polite conversation it's supposed to be a bad thing to talk about yourself; in public speaking, most of the time it's essential.

Let me give you a few of the samples of how Demosthenes used his new experience as a sea captain in crafting metaphors and images, painting pictures with words—something we will encounter with Chief Tecumseh of the Shawnee later on in our course—in order to grab the attention of his audience and help his own credibility.

> While the ship is in good condition, safe and undamaged, that is the time for the sailors and steersmen and the rest of the crew to take every precaution to safeguard it and protect it from being overturned by storms or sabotage. But once the ship has capsized, then it is too late for precaution. If we Athenians and the rest of the Greeks were overwhelmed by the lightning bolt that struck us [that is, Philip of Macedon and his armies], what action could we have taken? You might as well blame a ship's captain after his ship has been wrecked, even though he has taken every precaution and equipped his ship with everything that could help it pass safely through the sea. Yet the ship does run into a storm, and despite the captain's care its rigging is damaged or destroyed. But I was not the captain of our ship of state, nor was I in command as general, nor could I rule Fate. No, it was Fate that ruled all.

People remembered his words until their dying day; and that's another thing for you to consider as you plan your public speeches, be they short or long: Someone out there may find in what you say the words that crystallize a feeling, an event, a moment and remember them as the words of Demosthenes were remembered by his fellow countrymen. He had worked for that position; he had strived, he had struggled in order to become someone that people would admire, someone that people would remember.

In closer times than the fifth century B.C. to our own, we find other testimony to great speakers, both in the real world of history and in fiction, who do the same kind of preparation that Demosthenes undertook; and I'd like to consider a couple of those. One is someone you know very well: Abraham Lincoln. Abraham Lincoln, as we all know, loved books; and every time he had a chance to buy one he would go get that book and there by the firelight of his little cabin there in my state of Indiana, or later in Illinois, absorb what was in that book. But he had a favorite book: He had a book by a man named Scott that was called *Lessons in Elocution*. We're going to be hearing from this book as we go along; the important thing to know is it was both guides on how to present yourself and it was a book on presenting you with extracts from great speeches, some from Shakespeare's plays, some from history, or just short little after-dinner aphorisms and anecdotes that you could practice on. It was his constant companion. The sixth edition, printed in Concord, New Hampshire in 1820, was probably the one that he owned. He wore it out; and to the end of his days—even in his presidency—he loved to talk with people about the speeches of Shakespeare and what they could teach us about statesmanship, or diplomacy, or the efforts to be a leader. Lincoln, like Demosthenes, grew up in obscurity and tried to remedy that with work, systematic work, at studying speeches and oratory.

We find more testimony to this and pushing Elizabeth off her throne. He is going to meet, in this plan, wneed to work at it in, of all places, the novels of Jane Austen. In Austen's novel *Mansfield Park*, Jane Austen described a conversation between two brothers in a noble house—Tom and Edmund Bertram—about public speaking and how they were trained as boys by their father to be effective public speakers. They would memorize poems or speeches and deliver then there in the house while their father listened when they were home from their schools on holidays. This is part of an argument; the grownup brothers are engaged in a fight because Tom, the elder, wants to put on a play at home with his sisters acting very racy, somewhat sexually suggestive parts, and Edmund—who will one day be a clergyman—is very much opposed to this kind of private theatrical. Here is their conversation; this is Tom speaking first:

> Nobody is fonder of the exercise of talent in young people, or promotes it more, than my father, and for anything of the acting, spouting, reciting kind, I think he has always [had] a decided taste. I am sure he encouraged it in us as boys. How many a time have we mourned over the dead body of Julius Caesar, and to be'd and not to be'd, in this very room, for his amusement? And I am

> sure, my name was Norval, every evening of my life through one Christmas holidays.

Edmund disagrees:

> It was a very different thing. You must see the difference yourself. My father wished us, as schoolboys, to speak well, but he would never wish his grown-up daughters to be acting plays.

There we have a distinction based on gender lines: The boys of a great English house are expected to speak, whether as members of Parliament, justices of the peace, clergymen like Edmund, or—if there had been a third son—a soldier going into the military, needing to address the troops as an officer. The girls are meant to be seen but not heard in public. Today we expect everyone to be able to speak for themselves, especially in a democracy.

Let's recap the lessons we've learned today, and let's especially think of our hero, Demosthenes, the man who has led us into this world of public speaking and wants us to understand what will take us along the road in our first steps. First of his lessons: Make up your mind that you can and will overcome fears and obstacles. Second: Practice, practice, practice every aspect of public speaking. Third: Use crosstraining in acting, sports, and other fields to improve your skills. Fourth: Work on memorization. Fifth: Accept early failures and persist with your efforts. If you can take these initial steps, you will be following in the footsteps of Demosthenes himself, a man who had more obstacles against him—as far as pursuing a career in public speaking—than any other major historic figure known to us, and who yet, through his persistence and his belief in himself, overcame them all.

Practice Your Delivery—Patrick Henry

Lecture 2

Gentlemen may cry, Peace, Peace—but there is no peace. The war is actually begun! The next gale that sweeps from the north will bring to our ears the clash of resounding arms! Our brethren are already in the field! Why stand we here idle? What is it that gentlemen wish? What would they have? Is life so dear, or peace so sweet, as to be purchased at the price of chains and slavery? Forbid it, Almighty God! I know not what course others may take; but as for me, give me liberty or give me death!

—Patrick Henry, "Give Me Liberty or Give Me Death" speech

It's a fascinating fact that more of your impression on the audience is going to be made by the voice and the body than by the words themselves. You can completely undercut a great speech by reciting it in a monotone or by being uncertain and monotonous in your gestures and your delivery with your body. Nothing should ever happen that is not motivated by something in the words, but you will infinitely reinforce the impact of your words with proper use of the voice and the body.

We're going to turn to one of the giants of the American Revolution—Patrick Henry, who was speaking in the Virginia House of Burgesses in 1775 trying to get his fellow members to vote to join the Revolution. Patrick Henry gave the famous "Give Me Liberty or Give Me Death" speech in order to get Virginia off the fence and clearly behind the revolutionaries. Here are the words of an eyewitness who was in the House of Burgesses when Patrick Henry spoke on that day in 1775:

> The tendons of his neck stood out white and rigid like whipcords. His voice rose louder and louder until the walls of the building and all within them seemed to shake and rock in its tremendous vibrations. Finally his pale face and glaring eyes became terrible to look upon.

At the words "or give me death" at the end of his speech, Patrick Henry plunged an imaginary dagger into his heart and collapsed back into his seat. You have to be careful on the gestures; there were things that must have seemed dramatic and exciting in 1775 that might seem to us over the top. Nonetheless, it's very clear that what got people so excited was the theatricality of his delivery. When he finished, there was cheering, yelling, applauding, and an almost unanimous vote that Virginia would join the Revolution. A lot of the power came not from the words but from what that anonymous observer told us: the passionate action that put the words across.

Library of Congress, Prints & Photographs Division, LC-USZ62-102566.

Patrick Henry, whose impassioned speech inspired Virginia to join in the American Revolution.

The action of a speech has two parts: the voice and the body. Let's talk about the voice first. It may never have occurred to you how many elements make up your vocal production in terms of coloring the meaning and the emotion of every speech you make. There's volume, pitch, tone, pauses (that is, silence); there's also the pace at which you speak, the accents you put on individual words, and finally the inflection of a phrase. All of this is part of speech, and to some extent you need to be making conscious decisions about how you are going to inflect your words in order to give them the utmost meaning and force.

Volume is the easiest tool here: You have to use variety; you have to save the *forte* and the *piano*, the loud and the soft, for specific moments, or make your speech a crescendo, as Patrick Henry is said to have done with the "Give Me Liberty or Give Me Death" speech. Then there's pitch: You should vary the pitch from low to high, with most of the speech given in a comfortable middle range and high and low pitch used for dramatic value. The way to go after this, I believe, is cross-training through singing. I would recommend signing up for an amateur chorus or just singing in the shower. Singing will also help you think about enunciation, breath control, supporting your voice, and projecting your voice to a large crowd or in a big space.

In addition to voice, of course, we have the body. The most important part of your body as you speak is your eye. You may remember that Patrick Henry was famous for this: That observer that saw him give the "Liberty or Death" speech said, "He fixed the audience with a glare." He was trying to hold them fast, hold their attention. If you are looking straight into a person's eyes, it's very hard for them to look away, and the intensity of your meaning and your emotion will come through to them very clearly.

Beyond the eye, it's really the body that we're talking about. First rule: Stand up straight; make the most of your height, whatever it is. Standing straight suggests assurance, conviction, and pride; all of that needs to come across when you are speaking. Then there are the gestures: Remember that you shouldn't move unless it is inspired by or reinforcing a phrase or a word. Use your hands as you would in ordinary speech; don't work up a separate set of oratorical poses; simply make it seem natural. Your gestures and the movements of your body should all convince the audience you're alive. Nobody wound you up and pressed the On button; you're a human being like them, and the gestures will help reinforce that impression. ■

Take-Away Points

1. Use your voice and body language to reinforce your message.

2. Always match your voice and movements to specific words and emotions.

3. When you first start out as a speaker, mark the tone and gestures into your text as reminders; they are as important as the words themselves.

4. Establish and maintain eye contact with your audience.

5. In cases where you are not inciting a revolution, smile.

Practice Your Delivery—Patrick Henry

Lecture 2—Transcript

Welcome back. The hero of our first lecture on "The Art of Public Speaking" was Demosthenes of Athens. He was once asked by an admirer after he'd attained preeminence as the greatest public speaker in the known world, "What is the single most important element of public speaking?" Demosthenes answered, "Action." So they said again, "What is the second most important element?" and Demosthenes said, "Action." "And the third?" "Action."

What did Demosthenes mean by this word we translate "action?" In the Classical set of elements for good public speaking that was propounded by later speakers like Cicero in Rome, *pronuntiatio*, pronouncing your speech, was everything to do with delivery. In other words, not the text of the speech itself and not your own *elocutio*—or elocution in pronouncing it as we think of the word "pronouncing"—but the way you got your voice and your body into the speech; and it's amazing that Demosthenes, so focused on the words, so focused on the text, still thought voice and body language were the most important.

I mentioned in our first lecture that Demosthenes believed in crosstraining, and I talked to you about a couple of examples: the pebble in the mouth, a very odd sort of exercise, working on a sort of secondary point, the clear elocution of the words. He clearly wasn't going to speak in public with that pebble, but his voice would ever after be more attuned to exact pronunciation, clear enunciation of the words because of the pebble. The running up the hill, the shouting over the waves, this was athletics brought into the training for public speaking; and I do want to say, there's something about getting your body under your control that helps with public speaking. If you think about the number of times you've heard sports figures, male or female, on the television or on radio being interviewed, you have not heard any inarticulate ones. Whatever they may have to say, they feel very free and easy about saying it, and somehow the control of the body carries over; it is a form of crosstraining.

Demosthenes did crosstraining in a way that may seem very natural once you hear it: He studied with actors. Athens was famous for having great drama. It had giants like Sophocles, Aristophanes, and Euripides who'd written plays in the generations before Demosthenes was alive; these plays were classics now. He went down to the theater and he apprenticed himself to actors who could talk to him about tone of voice, dramatic pauses, gestures, stance—they didn't go into facial expression because they wore masks—but everything that could be conveyed by the way you were standing, the way you were moving, gestures with the hand, that's what he was studying. Also, how do you project your voice to thousands of people without amplification?

Cross-training is important to us as we focus today on our topic, which is the use of the voice, the use of the body to reinforce your meaning. It's a fascinating fact that more of your impression on the audience is going to be made by the voice and the body than by the words themselves. You can completely undercut a great speech by reciting it in a monotone, by ending every sentence as if it were a question, or by being uncertain and monotonous in your gestures and your delivery with your body. At some point, television commentators were told they should use their hands; and so a certain number of stock gestures happen again and again. Nothing should ever happen that is not motivated by something in the words, but you will infinitely reinforce the impact of your words with proper use of the voice and with proper use of the body.

We're going to turn to one of the giants of the American Revolution—the man who Thomas Jefferson said founded the Revolution—Patrick Henry, who was speaking to the Virginia House of Burgesses in 1775 trying to get his fellow members of the House to vote to join the Revolution. At this time it had begun in Massachusetts; everything depended on Virginia, the biggest and richest of the colonies, joining in. Patrick Henry gave the famous "Give Me Liberty or Give Me Death" speech in order to get Virginia off of its position of being on the fence and clearly behind the revolutionaries. By great good luck, we have a record from an eyewitness of what Patrick Henry looked like as he gave that speech and what he sounded like. Let's hear the words of an eyewitness; this was, in fact, a Baptist preacher who happened to be in St. John's Church on that day in 1775:

> The tendons of his neck stood out white and rigid like whipcords. His voice rose louder and louder until the walls of the building and all within them seemed to shake and rock in its tremendous vibrations. Finally his pale face and glaring eyes became terrible to look upon.

At the words "or give me death" at the end of his speech, Patrick Henry plunged an imaginary dagger into his heart and collapsed back into his seat. You have to be careful on the gestures; there were things that must have seemed dramatic and exciting in 1775 that might seem to us over the top. Nonetheless, it's very clear that what got people so excited was the sound, the theatricality, of his delivery; and as you will see when we go through a portion of his speech, he has built some of the elements into his own words, with lots of repetitions, which call for differences in delivery in order to be effective.

Here we go: We are in St. John's Church in Virginia; Patrick Henry, a young member, has risen to speak. He is already notorious for a speech that is remembered by us as the "If This Be Treason Make the Most of It" speech, so they're all braced for something powerful:

> I have but one lamp by which my feet are guided, and that is the lamp of experience. I know of no way of judging of the future but by the past. And judging by the past, I wish to know what there has been in the conduct of the British ministry for the last ten years to justify those hopes with which gentlemen have been pleased to solace themselves and the House. … If we wish to be free … we must fight! I repeat it, sir, we must fight! An appeal to arms and to the God of hosts is all that is left us!
>
> They tell us, sir, that we are weak; unable to cope with so formidable an adversary. But when shall we be stronger? Will it be the next week, or the next year? Will it be when we are totally disarmed, and when a British guard shall be stationed in every house? … Sir, we are not weak if we make a proper use of those means which the God of nature hath placed in our power. The millions of people, armed in the holy cause of liberty, and in such a country as that which

> we possess, are invincible by any force which our enemy can send against us. … The battle, sir, is not to the strong alone; it is to the vigilant, the active, the brave. … The war is inevitable—and let it come! I repeat it, sir, let it come.
>
> … Gentlemen may cry, Peace, Peace—but there is no peace. The war is actually begun! The next gale that sweeps from the north will bring to our ears the clash of resounding arms! Our brethren are already in the field! Why stand we here idle? What is it that gentlemen wish? What would they have? Is life so dear, or peace so sweet, as to be purchased at the price of chains and slavery? Forbid it, Almighty God! I know not what course others may take; but as for me, give me liberty or give me death!

When he finished, there was cheering, yelling, applauding, and an almost unanimous vote that Virginia would join the Revolution. A lot of the power came not from the words, good though they are, but from what that anonymous observer told us: the passionate action, that thing that Demosthenes referred to, that put the words across; and as I tried to point out, you heard how he wrote into his own speech elements that would lend themselves to varied expression. In particular, it's those repeated phrases and repeated words.

I'd like to stay on this one more moment with another example from a very different person—although equally a revolutionary—Oliver Cromwell, he who had Charles I beheaded after this king of England seemed to have betrayed the people's trust, he who then became Lord Protector himself, put in a Parliament, and then became so disgusted with that Parliament that he came down to the House of Commons and disbanded it in what is called the Dismissal of the Rump Parliament in 1653. We have it on record that after hearing them debating that they would extend their own term so they could continue to debate longer, he rose in a fury from his place, clapped his hat on his head, and began to stamp up and down, kicking and shouting at them the following words:

> … Ye are a factious crew and enemies to all good government; ye are a pack of mercenary wretches, and would like Esau sell your country for a mess of pottage, and like Judas betray your God for a

> few pieces of money. … Ye have no more religion than my horse; gold is your God; which of you have not barter'd your conscience for bribes? … you were deputed here by the people to get grievances redress'd, are become the greatest grievance. … I command ye therefore, upon the peril of your lives, to depart immediately out of this place; go, get you out! … In the name of God, go!

That was a section of a speech in which the "Go, get you gone!" was repeated again and again, each time, we can imagine, accompanied by the stamping of Cromwell's boots on the floor of the chamber; and what it made it so terrifying to all present was, of course, not the words, not the biblical invocations—which you heard were then later shared by Patrick Henry as they will be shared by Lincoln and many others—all that artistry would have been nothing without the forcefulness of that delivery.

As we look at this expression of voice and body that needs to accompany the words, we remember Demosthenes's "action." Action for him, remember, has two parts: the voice, the body. Let's talk about the voice first. It may never have occurred to you how many elements make up your vocal production in terms of coloring the meaning and the emotion of every speech you make. There's volume, pitch, tone, pauses (that is, silence); there's also the pace at which you speak, the accents you put on individual words, and finally the inflection of a phrase. All of this is part of speech, and to some extent you need to be making conscious decisions about how you are going to inflect your words in order to give them the utmost of meaning and force.

Let's start with volume, that's the easiest one: Just as in music there is *forte*, loud, like this; and there is *piano*, soft, like this. If you were to give an entire speech either softly or loudly, it would be intolerable. You have to use variety; you have to save the *forte* and the *piano*, the loud and the soft, for specific moments, or make your speech what a musician would call a crescendo, as Patrick Henry is said to have done with the "Give Me Liberty or Give Me Death" speech. Then there's pitch: I'd like to spend a bit of time on pitch, because it's what keeps our words literally from becoming monotonous. "Monotonous"—*mono-*, one; *tonos*, tone—means you stayed on one tone for the entire speech and believe me, it was monotonous. What you want to do is vary the pitch from low pitch to high pitch, with most of the speech given in a comfortable middle range but with high pitch and low pitch used for dramatic value.

I think we can get some instruction from Winston Churchill, one of the most famous orators of the 20th century, on this matter by looking and listening to a couple of clips where he is talking about issues to do with World War II; and in the first clip, I believe, is not setting us a good example. He's giving us a list of things at the beginning, and he's hitting the same high pitch again and again; it becomes somewhat monotonous, it would become much more forceful if he would vary the pitch. Let's listen:

> What kind of a people do they think we are? Is it possible they do not realize that we shall never cease to persevere against them until they have been taught a lesson which they and the world will never forget?

He got wild applause for that, but think how much more effective if would have been if he had not five times hit the same high note at the beginning; it almost begins to get into the way of your understanding the words if they are all put on the same pitch. Let's return to that great speaker, Winston Churchill, now for an example in how to use everything from high to low and how to put different words onto different pitches when he gets to his climax:

> It is not given to us to peer into the mysteries of the future. Still I avow my hope and faith, sure and inviolate, that in the days to come, the British and American people will for their own safety and for the good of all walk together in majesty, in justice, and in peace.

You could hear in that second clip, he was using those lower tones more frequently—I think that's always better, high pitch suggests tension in the vocal cords and fear on the part of the speaker—but he was also varying with some high stuff in the middle; and did you hear that fairly monotonous stuff to begin with, those lines where he kept the same pitch? That's to prepare you for an explosion of feeling and force and excitement as he begins to vary the pitch on every word.

The way to go after this, I believe, is crosstraining through singing. I love to sing; you may hate to sing, but singing can help you. I would recommend signing up for an amateur chorus or just singing in the shower, but thinking about the different pitches that you assign to the different words. Singing will also help you think about breath control, supporting your voice, projecting your voice to a large crowd or in a big space, and it will also make you think about enunciation; about the vowels and the consonants that make up your words. Crosstraining with singing, I believe, is a great tool.

I'd like to share with you one of my favorite passages from English poetry that a good composer has, I think, treated in a way that helps us see how you can learn to project words in speech even through singing. The poem is by Adelaide Proctor and it's called "The Lost Chord." It was set to music by Sir Arthur Sullivan, most famous for his work with Gilbert and Sullivan as the musical part of a partnership that produced the Savoy Operas. Here is Adelaide's poem:

> Seated one day at the organ,
> I was weary and ill at ease,
> And my fingers wandered idly
> Over the noisy keys;
> I know not what I was playing
> Or what I was dreaming then,
> But I struck one chord of music,
> Like the sound of a great Amen.

Sullivan, in his musical setting, starts as Churchill started when he was presenting that second speech in monotones to add force to the moment where every word, every syllable, gets its own different pitch.

> [Sings] Seated one day at the organ,
> I was weary and ill at ease,
> And my fingers wandered idly
> Over the noisy keys;
> I know not what I was playing
> Or what I was dreaming then,
> But I struck one chord of music,

Like the sound of a great Amen,
Like the sound of a great Amen.

Proctor doesn't repeat the last phrase, but Sullivan wanted to; and he made sure that he varied the pitches so there would be a sense of climax and newness to the expression.

That may have seemed like it didn't get to the greatest climax it could have; that's because we have a long way to go with this song. Sullivan is reserving, as you should when you give a speech, your climax for the most important point. The most important point is her last words:

It may be that Death's bright Angel,
Will speak in that chord again;
It may be that only in Heav'n,
I shall hear that grand Amen.

I don't have a high "C"; listen to Caruso singing this and you will hear the proper ending to Adelaide Proctor's "The Lost Chord." All of these lessons are actually more easily learned by singing than by continuing to speak and just trying to work on your pitch. Nonetheless, write some notes as you go into the text of your speech to remind yourself high, low, soft, loud; but especially when you want to pause. I often find that when I'm looking out at a big crowd and I somehow have gotten in a flow of words that hasn't let up for a while and the sound of my voice has been ceaseless, if I will simply pause the focus snaps together again. Sullivan knew that; every singer pauses before they hit his words "Amen" at the end of each of those phrases.

In addition to voice, of course, we have the body. The most important part of your body as you speak is your eye. You may remember that Patrick Henry was famous for this: That observer that saw him give the "Liberty or Death" speech said, "He fixed the audience with a glare." He was staring at them, he was not looking at a script; he was trying to hold them fast, hold their attention. If you are looking straight into a person's eyes it's very hard for them to look away and the intensity of your meaning and your emotion will come through to them very clearly. I often try to find a few sympathetic people in the audience who seem to be smiling or nodding and look at them, bouncing back and forth to the ones who seem to be in tune with the message; that helps me keep eye contact. But I also try to feel that at the end of every talk, even if there were a thousand in the hall, I hope everyone felt I was looking at them at some point. Work on that; it means that you're going to need to get free of the script, it means you're going to need to look up at times, it means ultimately ideally you'll either have the speech memorized—which I don't really recommend as a word for word thing—or feel free to more or less extemporize your speech. Winston Churchill once said he had to write everything down, he had to memorize it with all of its inflections, other people are able to, as he said, "fly on unpinioned wing," extemporize as they go; he admired that, but the result is the same in either case: You need to be able to look your audience straight in the eye.

Beyond that, beyond the eye, it's really the body, the limbs that we're talking about. First rule: Stand up straight; make the most of your height, whatever it is. You need to be standing tall, standing proud. Standing straight suggests assurance, conviction, pride; all of that needs to come across when you are speaking. Then there are the gestures: You shouldn't move unless it is inspired by or reinforcing a phrase or a word. If you have nothing exciting to illustrate, it's fine to just stand at attention and speak; but as soon as you begin to feel that there are specific words you want to emphasize, start using your hands. Use them as you would in ordinary speech; don't work up a separate set of oratorical poses, simply make it seem natural. Work with the rhythm of the words, reinforce the rhythm of the words; your gestures, the movements of your body should all convince the audience you're alive. Nobody wound you up and pressed the on button; you're a human being like them, and the gestures will help reinforce that impression.

I think we can get some amusement now out of Abraham Lincoln's old book, lessons on elocution, when we see that book go against its own lesson about matching the unique gestures and unique intonation to the specific words if we look on their suggestions, there were four illustrations: how you should stand when you're talking. Let's look at this bit of instruction and see what we can make of it: "First, I want to reiterate, a correct speaker does not make a movement of limb or feature for which he has not a reason."

But then they go on; they are talking now about the attitude—that is, the position—you should put yourself in when you are beginning to speak. This is what they say about the boy, the student, who is in this class on elocution:

> He should rest the whole weight of his body on the right leg; the other just touching the ground … The knees should be straight, and braced, and the body inclining … to the right … The right arm must then be held out, with the palm open, the fingers straight and close, the thumb almost as distant from them as it will go; and the flat of the hand neither horizontal nor vertical, but exactly between both. …
>
> When the pupil has pronounced one sentence … the hand, as if lifeless, must drop down to the side … and the body, without altering the place of the feet, poise itself on the left leg, while the left hand raises itself into exactly the same position as the right was before …

This seems to me a perfect example of what not to do with your body when talking. According to Scott's lessons, you are then supposed to alternate every sentence back and forth, left to right. I think one thing they were trying to get at here was to encourage the student not to be standing there at attention, lifelessly, staring straight ahead but to engage both sides of the fall. Nonetheless, this is not the way to do it.

Perhaps more congenial to us are the pages and pages that tell the would-be orator how he should compose his face and his expression, and also use gestures and the positions of the limbs and the body to convey a certain kind of meaning. My favorite one is cheerfulness: "Cheerfulness, adds a smile." I would say that should be your default setting. Even at a eulogy for a beloved dead member of the family, a smile is not out of place; and if you continually practice on letting a smile be your guide, be your standard expression, you will immediately draw your audience to you in sense of sympathy and mutual good feeling. Let's go on for a few more: Joy, clap the hands. Grief—I really wonder if this one was ever used—"beating the head; grovelling on the ground," "screaming," "weeping," "lifting the eyes." Remorse—this is after they caught you in that financial or sexual scandal—"casts down the countenance." Courage, "steady and cool, opens the countenance," the voice firm and even. Exhorting, as a general to his army—this one surprised me—"a kind, complacent look." Finally, intoxication: "eyes half shut," "an idiot smile," an "affected bravado," a heavy head.

We don't need to go quite that far, but all of these things can help us be more impressive public speakers. Don't forget, please, that you need to use your entire body, your entire vocal equipment in order to reinforce the words of your speech.

Let's sum up; we have a number of lessons that Patrick Henry and our other speakers are teaching us. First, use your voice and body language to reinforce your message. Second, always match your voice and movements to specific words and emotions. Third, at first when you start out as a speaker, mark the tone and gestures into your text as reminders; they are as important as the words themselves. Fourth, establish and maintain eye contact with your audience. Fifth—and this one's just for me—in cases where you are not inciting a revolution, smile.

Be Yourself—Elizabeth I to Her Army

Lecture 3

My own experience with talking about myself has been that it transformed my lectures, my pep talks as a coach, my explanations of how to do things in the field for students into something that they pay more attention to and that they see more clearly and that at the end we feel like more of a team.

In this lecture, we tackle one of the most important, but most neglected, aspects of public speaking: talking about yourself. There's a famous man in American history, Dale Carnegie, who trained hundreds, if not thousands, of people in the art of public speaking; and he always said that the single besetting sin of most beginners was to talk in abstractions and to talk in impersonal terms, ignoring his mantra that was, "Be yourself, and let your audience know who you are."

One great speaker who gives us an example of how you should bring yourself into your words is Queen Elizabeth I of England. We are going to follow her in her barge from her palace in London, down the River Thames, to Tilbury, where her army is assembling to try to fend off the most serious invasion threat her island has ever known, at least since the time of William the Conqueror half a millennium earlier: the threat of the Spanish Armada in 1588. It looked hopeless for England: Elizabeth's fleet was undermanned, underequipped, underfinanced. It was up to her to put some heart into those men, and she did it perhaps in the most surprising way possible: She did it by talking about herself.

Public speaking can make people better, because it gets them in touch with who they really are.

The key moment in her speech is when she confesses her sense of her own weakness: "I know I have the body of a weak and feeble woman." By taking that tack, Elizabeth has drawn them in, drawn their sympathies to her, opened herself up to them, admitted her weakness, and I'm sure created feelings of courage and determination in that army that she could have gotten in no other way. She is a model for us of how you tackle a very difficult situation. Opening up to people in public speaking, as in private life, is the way to establish a true relationship.

Queen Elizabeth I of England motivated her outnumbered troops by opening up about her personal weakness.

Queen Elizabeth talks about laying her own honor and life down in the dust, dying with them if necessary. She has pledged to them she will not run away, that their danger is her danger. Because she opened up about something that they must have all been wondering about—the feeling of fighting for a woman, a weak woman, not a soldier-king as they were used to with her father and her grandfather—she tackled what was on everyone's mind, and she made it a strength. If you will open up about weaknesses, if you will open up about failures, you, too, can create the feeling that out of these past failures and out of these inherent weaknesses and your struggle to overcome them comes strength that you can share with your listeners. It's a great way to get a crowd on your side.

There are lots of ways in which you can talk to people about yourself. It doesn't have to be just weaknesses; it can be personal things to you that help people understand you. In fact, I think public speaking can make people better, because it gets them in touch with who they really are; it puts them in a forum where they can say anything about themselves and know that it will only add to the sense of authenticity, of communication, of revelation, and finally of communication with the audience. Nobody's perfect; we all feel closer to people who we know through and through and who have felt confident enough to share their weaknesses and failures with us. ■

Take-Away Points

1. Explain your personal connection to the subject of your speech.

2. Share your own emotions, beliefs, and ideas, and don't shy away from revealing your weaknesses and failures.

3. Establish a personal link with your listeners at the start of your speech.

4. Use plain, direct language, but never talk down to your audience.

5. Don't hesitate to read your speech from a script if necessary.

6. Make sure that your audience will be able to hear you.

Be Yourself—Elizabeth I to Her Army

Lecture 3—Transcript

Welcome back. In this lecture, we are going to tackle one of the most important, but most neglected, aspects of public speaking: talking about yourself. There's a famous man in American history, Dale Carnegie, who trained hundreds, if not thousands, of people in the art of public speaking; and he always said that the single besetting sin of most beginners was to talk in abstractions and to talk in impersonal terms, ignoring his mantra that was, "Be yourself, and let your audience know who you are." I'd like you to think back to Patrick Henry, standing there in Saint John's Church, and ending his fiery revolutionary speech with a message that was from his heart and really very much about him: "I know not what course others may take; but as for me, give me liberty or give me death!" He was separating himself apart from that crowd; he was speaking from the heart, he was hoping others would follow, but he was really throwing down the gauntlet in the most personal way possible.

We're going to be looking at some great speakers today who give us examples of how you should bring yourself into your words; how you should share your feelings, even your weaknesses and failures, with the audience if you want to make the deepest connection possible with them. Our chief guest professor today is Queen Elizabeth I of England; we are going to follow her in her barge from her palace in London, down the River Thames, to Tilbury, where her army is assembling to try to fend off the most serious invasion threat her island has ever known, at least since the time of William the Conqueror half a millennium earlier: The threat of the Spanish Armada.

The year is 1588. The king of Spain, King Philip, has put together one of the largest fleets that the medieval and Renaissance world has ever known, with the idea of supporting Catholics in the country, and with a duke—the Duke of Parma, an Italian duke who is in the service of the king of Spain—pushing Elizabeth off her throne. It looked hopeless for England. It was up to her to put some heart into those men; and she did it perhaps in the most surprising way possible: She did it by talking about herself. Let's listen to her own words, and let's imagine the scene. She apparently read this speech—there's no reason to think that she didn't write it herself; it's very much of apiece with all of her discourses to her people—but she knew her voice was too weak to be heard all around the camp where they were all gathered, so she had copies made and captains read it out to their troops in every part of the field simultaneously. It was sort of an ancient PA system; but it worked very well, and it made everyone feel that they were really hearing from the queen herself.

> My loving people, we have been persuaded by some that are careful of our safety, to take heed how we commit our selves to armed multitudes, for fear of treachery. But I assure you, I do not desire to live to distrust my faithful and loving people. Let tyrants fear. … I am come amongst you as you see at this time, not for my recreation and disport, but being resolved, in the midst and heat of the battle, to live or die amongst you all, to lay down for my God, and for my kingdom, and for my people, my honour and my blood, even in the dust. I know I have the body of a weak and feeble woman, but I have the heart and stomach of a king, and of a king of England too, and think foul scorn that Parma, or Spain, or any Prince of Europe should dare to invade the borders of my realm, to which, rather than any dishonour shall grow by me, I myself will take up arms, I myself will be your general, judge, and rewarder of every one of your virtues in the field. I know already for your forwardness you have deserved rewards and crowns, and we do assure you, in the word of a Prince, they shall be duly paid you. … By your valour in the field, we shall shortly have a famous victory over those enemies of my God, of my kingdom, and of my people.

I want you to consider how strange a speech this is coming from a commander-in-chief where the key moment is when she confesses her sense of her own weakness: "I know I have the body of a weak and feeble woman." By taking that tack, Elizabeth has drawn them in, drawn their sympathies to her, opened herself up to them, admitted her weakness, and I'm sure created feelings of courage and determination in that army that she could have gotten in no other way. She is a model for us of how you tackle a very difficult situation. You are wanting to win sympathy, you are wanting people to know you right away, you are wanting people to believe in the same cause that you believe in; it's often not the right thing to just talk about how strong and how great you are. Opening up to people in public speaking as in private life is the way to establish a true relationship.

This may have been the first time that a reigning queen of England had ever taken her forces into the field as commander-in-chief. She was, in fact, not going to go on board the ships along with Sir Francis Drake and her other famous captains, she would wait on shore; but she doesn't let you see that in the speech. She talks about laying her own honor and life down in the dust, dying with them if necessary; and what she's looking forward to is that dreaded moment when the enemy might come ashore: She has pledged to them she will not run away, their danger is her danger. Because she opened up about something that they must have all been wondering about—the feeling of fighting for a woman, a weak woman, not a soldier-king as they were used to with her father and her grandfather—she tackled what was on everyone's mind and she made it a strength. If you will open up about weaknesses, if you will open up about failures, you, too, can create the feeling that out of these past failures and out of these inherent weaknesses and your struggle to overcome them comes strength that you can share with your listeners. It's a great way to get a crowd on your side.

I remember hearing an incredibly inspiring sermon; of all the hundreds of sermons I've heard in my life in churches, it's the one that certainly sticks with me most. It was by a Reverend George Mackey who was the minister at our church in New Albany, Indiana when I was small; a man who had grown up it seems in an odor of sanctity, of always doing the right thing, he was sort of the pillar of rectitude. But one day he gave a sermon about when he was bad; when he had failed to be a loving person. He'd been in the school where all of the future ministers were being taught, the seminary, and he was part of a group of healthy young fellows who liked to throw the ball around and go on long hikes. There was one young man in the group they picked on because he was weak, he had no stamina, he didn't join in their games; so they pushed him around, they mocked him, they made jokes about him. One day they were crossing the courtyard on a cold winter night, snow on the ground, and he was overtaken with a fit of coughing as he seemed to often be; and somebody made a joke about it and Mister Mackey, among others, laughed. Then they saw that there were spatters of pink and red on the snow; he was coughing blood. This young man had tuberculosis; he probably would not live long enough to be the minister that he wanted to be. But he was there, putting up with all their abuse, putting up with their mockery because he felt that was, whatever might happen, his mission in life. That was obviously a life changing experience for my minister; but hearing that story from someone I thought was perfect was a life changing experience for me.

There are lots of ways in which you can talk to people about yourself. It doesn't have to be just weaknesses; it can be personal things to you that help people understand you. I want to take another example of a great public speaker, and another great woman in history, Sojourner Truth. She was a slave in America, freed before the Civil War, who when the Civil War was over felt that the big war still lay ahead: equal rights for women. In 1867, she attended the national convention of American Equal Rights Association in the church of the Puritans in New York City; so she's talking to a friendly audience. She opened up about herself and her past and her feelings about the future:

> I am above eighty years old; it is about time for me to be going. I have been forty years a slave and forty years free, and would be here forty years more to have equal rights for all. [She was almost right; if she could have lived all the way to 1920 she would have seen the equal rights for women that she was hoping for.] I suppose I am kept here because something remains for me to do [that sense of incompleteness; a job not yet done; something that is a mission that she has not yet succeeded in]; I suppose I am yet to help to break the chain. I have done a great deal of work; as much as a man, but did not get so much pay. I used to work in the field and bind grain, keeping up with the cradler; but men doing no more, got twice as much pay … We do as much, we eat as much, we want as much. I suppose I am about the only colored woman that goes about to speak for the rights of the colored women. I want to keep the thing stirring, now that the ice is cracked.

You can tell, just from that short excerpt, what a powerful public speaker she is. She uses images in a terrific way, as we'll see in a later lecture when we follow the Shawnee chief Tecumseh on his speechmaking tours as he tries to unite all of the tribes. She has that gift, talking about "now that the ice is cracked" or "I want to stay here to help break the chain" of painting a picture in your mind so you remember things. But you also remember her: She uses pictures from her past life to make it vivid to you (and to me), and the phrase here that just brings this little excerpt to life for me is when she's describing herself in the field and what she's really emphasizing is the half pay for the same amount of work; but she can't give up on trying to convey to us how proud she is that in that drudgery, in that hard labor in the southern sun where she would go along and gather up the grain and bind it in sheaves, she was following the man with the rake who, as they say, was the cradler, who brought it together in rows, she kept up with him.

That little phrase "keeping up with the cradler" is that significant detail about herself, about personal experience, something that probably nobody else in that New York church knew anything about, that helps give this a feeling of authenticity. That's something we always want to see in personal dialogues, in personal communications and confessions: the feeling of authenticity. It's something, I think, that public speaking can do for you. In fact, I think public speaking can make people better, because it gets them in touch with who they are really; it puts them in a forum where they can really say anything about themselves and know that it will only add to the sense of authenticity, of communication, of revelation, and finally of communication with the audience. Nobody's perfect; we all feel closer to people who we know through and through and who have felt confident enough to share their weaknesses and failures with us.

We have people who have used their public speaking for statements of personal creed. One of these we're going to be visiting later on in our series of our guest lecturers, and that is Mahatma Gandhi, who in the 20th century was on trial for his life. we're going to be visiting him for an entire spell, an entire session, making him our chief guide; but I want to sort of prefigure his appearance with us later on with just the opening of that speech, which I think is so profoundly personal and not only made an important statement for his judge—his English judge there in India as he's on trial for his life—but also to the millions that he knew would be reading or listening to his words: "Non-violence is the first article of my faith. It is the last article of my faith. But I had to make my choice." With that short beginning, he has said an essential thing about the kind of person he is. I also want you to notice the simplicity, plainness, and directness of his language—something he shares with Queen Elizabeth and with Sojourner Truth—in trying to open himself up so that you will understand him, you will understand what means more to him than anything else on earth.

As an example of the wrong way to present yourself in a speech, I would like to present the Emperor Napoleon, who took leave of his Old Guard there in France in 1814 after a series of defeated by a great army of allies; they had captured Paris, and he was about to be sent away to the island of Elba in exile. He voluntarily surrendered; he did not fight to the death either for himself or for this Old Guard, who certainly would have followed him anywhere. Let's hear Napoleon, standing there in Paris, the Old Guard drawn up again for one last time in front of him, as he explains to them his feelings at this moment. These are soldiers he has been with for decades; he's bidding them farewell.

> Soldiers of my Old Guard! I bid you farewell. For twenty years I have constantly accompanied you on the road to honor and glory.

I want to say to you right now, this is a great start. That image of the monarch, the emperor, the general accompanying the troops—that they are the real leaders and he is just following in their slipstream—that is a tremendously powerful and moving way for the man who was briefly the most powerful human being on earth to talk to the soldiers who really made it all possible. The focus is on them, but they are getting the sense that he's opening up his heart to them and through his own feelings, his own vision of himself, really creates a feeling of pride in these men who have, in fact, suffered a very grievous defeat. But things start to go off the rails pretty quickly:

> In these latter times, as in the days of our prosperity, you have invariably been models of courage and loyalty. With men such as you our cause could not be lost; but the war would have been interminable; it would have been civil war, and that would have entailed deeper misfortunes on France.

We're getting a little torturous here; in his effort to try to pay them a compliment, to call them invincible when they have in fact been beaten, he is beginning to have to do mental gymnastics that are clouding the issue, clouding that straightforward emotion that he started with so very effectively. But now we really go the wrong way; right after saying this would have entailed deeper misfortunes on France, Napoleon goes on:

> I have sacrificed all my interests for my country.

Where did that come from? Suddenly the emphasis and the focus are on the speaker in the wrong way. He's wanting pity, he's wanting to be admired; he's no longer thinking about them except as an audience for his own revelations about how important he thinks he is and how wonderful he thinks he's been doing.

> I go, but you, my friends, will continue to serve France. Her happiness was my only thought. It will still be the object of my wishes. Do not regret my fate [we're on Broadway shows here with "Don't Cry for Me Argentina"; this is bathos, that over the top kind of emotionalism that starts to seem inappropriate and ridiculous]; if I have consented to survive, it is to serve your glory.

What? He explains what he means:

> I intend to write the history of the great achievements we have performed together. Adieu, my friends. Would I could press you all to my heart.

It's a good ending from "Adieu, my friends" onward; but again, the idea that somebody has consented to survive when he had all along been saying, "We will fight to the death," and then he's doing it so he can go off to a place of comparative safety and write a book about what they all did together, this is really descending from the sublime to the ridiculous. He was a monomaniac, there's no doubt about it, and he's not in the category of those first three speakers we heard; but as we consider that we have two absolute monarchs here, Elizabeth I and Napoleon, we see how Elizabeth expresses through her own willingness to open up genuine feelings about herself and say nothing that's not true about this problem—that she has the body of a weak and feeble woman—she gets the sympathy of the crowd and the sympathy of posterity. Napoleon, although this is printed and reprinted as a great speech, seems to me to say much more about himself then he does about the men that he is supposed to be praising and exalting.

My own experience with talking about myself has been that it transformed my lectures, my pep talks as a coach, my explanations of how to do things in the field for students into something that they pay more attention to and that they see more clearly and that at the end we feel like more of a team. I can remember the class notes and evaluations that I received in the semester that I finally decided I was going to stop simply turning the textbook into lectures and use illustrations from my own fieldwork and that of other people I'd worked with at the University of Louisville to tell the students a sort of story about what they were going to hear based on my own personal experiences. Immediately I found in the evaluations, "What I most like was hearing about my professor's own experiences." This gave me validity; this was an authentication of what made it valuable for them to be listening to me. This is always the question you have to think about when you are trying to convince people that you are worth listening to: Why me? What can I bring to this topic?

I admit I have it easy: If I am giving a pep talk as a rowing coach, I used to be a rower; I can talk about those experiences. If I am talking about archaeology in a lecture in a college classroom, I can talk about my own fieldwork and my own discoveries. But one thing I try to do is follow Elizabeth's example and talk about my mistakes and make it plain to them that they're going to need to learn from their own mistakes. I'm very interested in the fact that we often want nothing but success. The image that I like to use in class is that of a baby learning to walk: You cannot learn to walk from reading the books, studying the manuals, watching other people do it; you have to get out there and do it yourself and you have to fall down. Nobody walks without falling down, and that's true of most enterprises in life; nobody becomes an archaeologist without making mistakes. How do I illustrate this point about being willing to make mistakes? I talk to them about some of my own stupidities in the field. I'll give you an example.

The first time I was put in charge of a field team there in the Louisville area—I'd come back to town with my Cambridge Ph.D. in hand, very puffed up about myself—I'd been given the job simply because that particular survey required that the director be a Ph.D. I was the least experienced person in the field, if not in terms of all of things necessary to do a dig, certainly in terms of that area; I had never worked in Jefferson County, Kentucky as an archaeologist, my field crew had been working there for years. Did I sit down humbly and talk to them about it? No. When we were assigned areas to survey, did I go around to the different farmhouses, say that I knew nothing about the area but I would be grateful for information? No. Did I even take the trouble to go back through the records of previous archaeologists and study what they had found there? No. I was set up for a fall, and I got one.

There was a mound that we discovered back in some woods. I had, at that stage, always the dream that the next thing that would happen to me would be the *Time* magazine cover because this extraordinary prehistoric mound had been found and the team from the University of Louisville would have excavated it and brought to light these things that rewrote the history books. That was my dream, here was a big mound; most of the mounds in Jefferson County were destroyed a long time ago, and so this seemed like a chance to find something unique. I discovered that nobody else in the group was very excited about this; they had seen similar things. I was convinced this was a real prehistoric mound, it was sort as big as three haystacks piled on top of each other; and so I made them settle down for three days in over 100-degree heat and about 98 percent humidity. We stripped the shrubs and saplings off the top of that mound, no there's no shade to hide you from the hot noonday sun. We worked down in these textbook layers, and after three days one of them pulled up from the mound a bicycle chain and said, "Was this the prehistoric artifact you were looking for?" One minute later, we got a piece of plate glass and a brick.

I was shaken; so I finally did what I should have done in the beginning: I went to the nearest farmhouse—I could have seen the roof the whole time—knocked on the door and asked about the mound in the woods. I was told by the farmer's wife: "That's not a mound. That's the big pile of dirt that my husband pulled up out of the creek with his backhoe when he was trying to channelize the creek so it would flow better and we wouldn't get floods in the fields. That's just the stuff that he piled up." My name was Mud for a long time, and they all enjoyed laughing at me about it. But I learned a lot—I approach every field experience differently now—I learned in a way that I could only have learned from a failure, from a mistake, from making a fool of myself and I now have a story to tell to my students about my own mistake that can help them be ready for the inevitable mistakes they will make themselves.

I learned a lot from a series of speakers that we brought to the University of Louisville and the way that they would present themselves to our students, to the community at large. We had figures like Jane Goodall who would come, who would always begin by talking about her own vision, her own childhood, how she got into the field, her work with the chimpanzees, what it meant to her; and by the end of hearing her talk about it, there was nothing you wanted more than to join with this seemingly frail woman who had braved the outback in Africa, who had done more to create a new scientific field—primatology—than any other worker, but had done it all with this spirit of modesty, this spirit of grace and quiet, that was an entirely new thing in our lives. Sure, the points she was making about the necessity for conservation are good points; but what moved us was her own personal vision, her own story.

I remember going to a second lecturer, a second visitor, his name was Bob Ballard, a big man in my field of shipwreck studies; he's the man who had found the *Titanic*. How did he begin his speech? Did he talk about the excitement of the day, the heroic moment when the *Titanic* was discovered there two-and-a-half miles down in the North Atlantic and all those mysteries were finally solved? No, he talked about his childhood in Kansas, the most landlocked part of America, how he yearned even as a child to have something to do with the sea and how this *Titanic* and its discovery was the fulfillment of a dream that went all the way back to the time he was a little boy. What we took away from it was an image of a very human person for whom this discovery was a triumph, the kind of triumph we could all identify with.

Let's sum up what we've learned from Queen Elizabeth I, from our other speakers today; first, a set of lessons about being yourself, as Dale Carnegie said: First, explain your personal connection to the subject of your speech. You must have one; figure out what it is, and let your audience know. Second, share your own emotions, beliefs, and ideas, and don't shy away from revealing your weaknesses and failures. Third, establish a personal link with your listeners at the start of your speech. Think how Elizabeth I did that when she said her advisors had told her, "Don't go out in the crowd for fear of treason," and she said, "I would rather not live than distrust you"; there's a personal link. Fourth, use plain, direct language, but never—even if you are a monarch—talk down to your audience. Finally, a couple of general points that we get from Elizabeth: Fifth, don't hesitate to read your speech from a script if necessary; it can still be a very powerful experience for your audience. Finally, always make sure that your audience will be able to hear you, because believe me: If you are opening up yourselves to them they will want to hear every word.

Find Your Humorous Voice—Will Rogers

Lecture 4

The actress Meryl Streep pointed out one of the reasons why you need to be careful in deciding where you want to go in this realm of humor. Once when she was accepting an award or a tribute, she reflected back on a recent film that she had made where she had played for almost the first time a comic part and, laughing herself, ruefully she said, "Dying is easy. Comedy is hard."

One of the things to think about in preparing yourself to become a public speaker is humor, jokes. This is a very personal choice that you have to make, and in many societies it wouldn't arise, because many societies do not equate giving a public speech with telling jokes. Our obsession with the idea that if you're going to stand up you're probably going to need to be funny is a very old one in the English-speaking world. But you need to be careful with humor. You can't tell what effect your jokes will havc on a given group; often you will offend people more than you please them with a joke or with a satirical story; it's like a minefield when you get out there on that humorous terrain. Yet many audiences expect it, and I will tell you this: There's nothing that unifies an audience more than laughter. If you feel it in you to use jokes and to use humor, this is one more element you can put in your arsenal of tools as you start to approach your work as a speaker.

Library of Congress, Prints & Photographs Division, LC-USZ62-20553.

Will Rogers was a master at using comedy to focus attention on the substance of his speech.

American humorist Will Rogers started as a standup comedian. He had a very good career in films and was highly respected in America—so much so that, as we will see, he was invited by Columbia University to be an after-dinner speaker at a very important event.

The year was 1924; Columbia, with its president, Butler, had invited lots of their biggest donors, all of them alumni, to come to the college. Here is an excerpt:

> President Butler paid me a compliment in mentioning my name in his introductory remarks this evening. … I am glad he did that, because I got the worst of it last week. The Prince of Wales, in speaking of the sights of America, mentioned the Woolworth Building, the subway, the slaughterhouse, Will Rogers, and the Ford factory. He could at least put me ahead of the hogs.

We can see in his complete speech all the different kinds of humor that he brings in without ever—as we might think he would put it—stooping to tell a simple joke. He starts, deadpan, with a long section about being thankful to President Butler for mentioning his name at the opening ceremony and his gratitude because he was badly treated, as he thought, by the Prince of Wales. We expect a joke coming but we're still not getting it, and then we start to sense it when we understand the charge that he's making against the Prince of Wales: that this visitor, in listing the sites of America, mentioned the Woolworth building, the subway, the slaughterhouse, Will Rogers, and the Ford factory. Pretty honorable mention to be in that company; but I'm sure there was a big pause there while he let the audience try to work out what was coming, and then he used the brand of humor that involves crudeness and low language in a setting where you expect everything to be prim and proper with his sentence, "He could at least put me ahead of the hogs." Especially mentioning hogs at a dinner is something that seems a little incongruous and that low language, that crudeness—very mild, certainly in our eyes, but stronger back in 1924—must have gotten his first big laugh of the evening.

Will Rogers is playing the part of a court jester.

I want to point out something about the nature of this humor: Will Rogers is playing the part of a court jester—something we're all familiar with from the Middle Ages—that privileged person who is allowed to entertain the company with jokes made at members of the company that would be completely unacceptable in a normal social setting. The jester can get away with it because it's under the cloak of humor, and the laughter is felt to be in that same realm of laughter that we consider the special province of roasts, those ceremonial dinners where someone is toasted with jokes and barbs and witticisms at their expense. He's doing that same thing at these men who are, in fact, the guests of honor at the dinner because they are the men who've given all that money to Columbia.

We have here some techniques of comedy—the buildup, the surprise, the incongruity, the hyperbole—all of which are things that Will Rogers is a master of; but please notice, every single laugh that he evokes is making a point, every laugh is helping to focus attention on the real substance of his speech. Will Rogers was the right man for President Butler to invite if he wanted a memorable speech. Most after-dinner speeches are imminently forgettable; I'm sure the people who were there in Columbia University's dining hall in 1924 remembered this for the rest of their lives, even if the jokes were at their expense. ■

Take-Away Points

1. Laugh at yourself before you laugh at others.

2. Comedy helps relax your audience, especially at formal occasions.

3. Use humor to focus on your theme, not to distract from it.

4. Jokes can illuminate serious points, providing new thoughts and perspectives.

5. Your humor should reflect your own personality.

6. Nothing unifies an audience quicker than laughter.

Find Your Humorous Voice—Will Rogers

Lecture 4—Transcript

Welcome back. In this lecture, we're going to wrap up our first section of the course on public speaking, that section that we have devoted to preparing yourself to become a public speaker. We've covered things like Demosthenes with his crosstraining of athletic work and studying with actors, his determination to get over those speech impediments; we've also talked about our need to develop voice and body language control so that we can really make the best of our delivery as we deliver our speech; and then, just last time, we were talking about how you need to get personal in your speeches. As it said on the Temple at Delphi in Greece that I study as an archaeologist: [Greek], "Know thyself," and I would go on to say, "And put yourself into your speech."

We're concluding our quartet of opening lectures with one about humor, one about jokes. This is a very personal choice that you have to make, and in many societies it wouldn't arise, because many societies do not equate giving a public speech with telling jokes. But I have at home a little leather-bound volume printed in the mid-18th century, which is a tiny crib book that a gentleman could carry in his pocket to a dinner where he might have to make an after-dinner speech; it was to give him, ready to hand, a whole selection of anecdotes, jokes, humorous pieces on all sorts of different subjects so that he could shine as a speaker. Our obsession with the idea that if you're going to stand up you're probably going to need to be funny is a very old one in the English-speaking world. But we know that other societies don't feel the same way. A friend of mine, who is a great enthusiast for Japanese art, told me a funny story about going to a conference of Japanese-American culture where the speaker stood up and said to all of this assembled group, some Japanese and some American, "In America, it is customary to open a speech with a joke; in Japan, it is customary to start every speech with an apology. I shall pay attribute to both traditions: I shall start my speech with an apology for not knowing any jokes." It got a big laugh, it got things off, but it pointed out that this interest that we have in the English-speaking world for jokes and humor in public speaking is not universal.

The actress Meryl Streep pointed out one of the reasons why you need to be careful in deciding where you want to go in this realm of humor. Once when she was accepting an award or a tribute, she reflected back on a recent film that she had made where she had played for almost the first time a comic part and, laughing herself, ruefully she said, "Dying is easy. Comedy is hard." She's right; you can't tell what effect your jokes will have on a given group; often you will offend people more than you please them with a joke or with a satirical story; it's like a minefield when you get out there on that humorous terrain. Yet many audiences expect it; and I will say this now and we're going to come back to this at the end of the lecture: There's nothing that unifies an audience more than laughter. If you feel it in you to use jokes and to use humor, I would say this is that last element you're going to want to think of as you put together your arsenal of tools as you start to approach your work as a comic speaker, if that's what you're going to be; but any kind of speaker, you may want to use this element, but you need to think about it in advance, and you need to use it.

I myself am one of those people that falls into the category of that man we just talked about who made the joke saying, "I'm going to apologize for not knowing any jokes"; I'm not quite that bad, I know one. I'm going to tell it to you now; we'll revisit it at the end, you can decide during the time between now and when we get to it what possible application there could be for me, an archaeologist, in using this joke in every course I teach. I don't know what is wrong with my DNA, I don't know what's wrong with my mental processes; jokes slip off my mind—and I've heard thousands—as food slips off Teflon; I just can't retain them. But I remember this one:

> It's a dark night. A policeman turns a street corner and sees in front of him on the pavement, in the pool of light under a lamppost, a man on his hands and knees desperately feeling around on the pavement as if he's lost something that's a matter of life or death. The policeman says to the man, "Sir, what's happened? What's wrong?" and the man says, "I lost my wallet." "Let me help you," says the policeman, and he gets down on his hands of knees; and in a short time they've covered every square inch of that pavement, and the gutter, and the base of the lamppost, right out to the rim of the light, and the policeman stands up, a little confused, and says,

> "Sir, where did you lose this wallet?" The man points to a dark alley well down the block and says, "I lost it over there." "Then why are you looking here?" The man answers, "Well, the light's better here."

Believe it or not, that has a serious archaeological message; I'm not sure it would fit into everyone's career as a joke that makes a point, but it does in mine. It's the only one I can remember. It always does get a laugh; I tell it at the beginning of my classes, and I get that laughter, that ripple of unanimous mirth that makes me feel the class is kind of pulled together around that joke. We'll come back later on and look at its meaning.

What I want to do now is introduce you to our guest lecturer for today, American humorist Will Rogers. Will Rogers was a man who started as a standup comedian, had a very good career in films, and was highly respected in America; so much that, as we will see, he was invited by Columbia University to be an after-dinner speaker at a very important event. The year was 1924; Columbia, with its president, Butler, in charge, had invited lots of their biggest donors, all of them alumni, to come to the college. They were actually honoring an old alumnus, Alexander Hamilton, who, of course, as a treasurer of the United States was the right man to be honoring if you're going to talk about money; and when Will Rogers published this speech—and he almost never published his after-dinner addresses, they were off the cuff and not meant for posterity—he called it "Education and Wealth." Here we go:

> President Butler paid me a compliment in mentioning my name in his introductory remarks this evening. ... I am glad he did that, because I got the worst of it last week. The Prince of Wales, in speaking of the sights of America, mentioned the Woolworth Building, the subway, the slaughterhouse, Will Rogers, and the Ford factory. He could at least put me ahead of the hogs.
>
> Everything must be in contrast at an affair like this. You know to show anything off, you must have contrast. Now, I am here tonight representing poverty. We have enough wealth right here at this table, right here at the speaker's table alone—their conscience should

> hurt them, which I doubt if it does—so that we could liquidate our national debt. Every rich man reaches a time in his career when he comes to a turning point and starts to give it away. I have heard that of several of our guests here tonight, and that is one of the reasons I am here. I would like to be here for the psychological moment. …
>
> I'm not here to keep cool with Coolidge, but to praise President Butler. Columbia was nothing twenty years ago. Now, President Butler has gone around and got over a hundred buildings, and has annexed Grant's Tomb. Butler was the first man to go around to the graduates and explain to them that by giving money to Columbia it would help on the income tax and also perpetuate their names. … [Columbia] is the foremost university. There are thirty-two hundred courses. You spend your first two years in deciding what course to take, the next two years in finding the building that these courses are given in, and the rest of your life in wishing you had taken another course.

That's about two-thirds of Will Rogers's speech, but it's enough to show us all the different kinds of humor that he brings in without ever—as we might think he would put it—stooping to tell a simple joke; one of those jokes that are impersonal, something not about himself, not about the occasion, but a joke with a punch line that people listen to and then burst out laughing at the incongruity or whatever it may be that is the source of the humor. I'd like to go back through this speech a little bit and look at the different forms of humor and the different lessons we can get from it.

He starts, deadpan, with a long section about being thankful to President Butler for mentioning his name at the opening ceremony and his gratitude because he was badly treated, as he thought, by the Prince of Wales. We expect a joke coming but we're still not getting it, and then we start to sense it when we understand the charge that he's making against the Prince of Wales: that this foreign visitor, in listing the sites of America, mentioned the Woolworth building, the subway, the slaughterhouse, Will Rogers, and the Ford factory. Pretty honorable mention to be in that company; but I'm sure there was a big pause there while he let the audience try to work out what was coming, and then he used the brand of humor that involves crudeness and low language in a setting where you expect everything to be prim and proper with his sentence, "He could at least put me ahead of the hogs." Especially mentioning hogs at a dinner is something that seems a little incongruous and that low language, that crudeness—very mild, certainly in our eyes, but stronger back in 1924—must have gotten his first big laugh of the evening.

He then goes on for another setup; it's not a string of punch lines, everything has to be set up. You can almost hear in this speech the pauses and the shifts of gear where he's moving into his next setup for that next punch line. Everything must be in contrast at an affair like this. To show anything off, you must have contrast; that's a simple truth, it almost rates as another thing that used to be part of every speech: platitudes; something that everybody would agree on, a sort of self-evident proposition that every speaker felt safe in making. But he's about to explode the platitudinous mood with: "I am here tonight representing poverty." That's a funny thing to do; we talked about Queen Elizabeth exposing her weaknesses to view, now Will Rogers is going to show you what he feels is his weakness, his Achilles heel: He's a poor man. That's not the contrast yet; what is in contrast to him? The fact that "We have enough wealth right here at this table, right here at the speaker's table alone"—note the repetition for emphasis; he's bringing them on board, he's building up that crescendo—and then a little parenthetical phrase: "their conscience should hurt them, which I doubt if it does—so that we could liquidate our national debt." I bet that got a big laugh, because it probably wasn't far off from the truth. Columbia's graduates and alumni at that time numbered some of the most important and some of the richest men in America; they might have been able to make a dent in the national debt.

I want to point out something here about the nature of this humor: Will Rogers is playing the part of a court jester—something we're all familiar with from the Middle Ages—that privileged person who is allowed to entertain the company with jokes made at members of the company that would be completely unacceptable in a normal social setting; but that jester can get away with it, because it's under the cloak of humor and the laughter is felt to be in that same realm of laughter that we consider the special province of roasts, those ceremonial dinners where someone is toasted with jokes and barbs and witticisms at their expense. He's doing that same thing at these men who are, in fact, the guests of honor at the dinner because they are the men, as you remember, who've given all that money so Columbia can grow as it's grown with all these new buildings.

He wants to set up, again, our next joke, so we go on with, "Every rich man reaches a time in his career when he comes to a turning point and starts to give it away." I think probably people laughed at almost anything Will Rogers said, but that's not humorous in itself; it's part of the setup, it's a platitude in a way. But he is going to be able to laugh at these people now, freely, partly because—I want you to remember back—the first laugh was at himself. He's laughing now at these rich men—"they could liquidate the national debt"; "I think their conscience should bother them, I don't think it does"—he's laughing at them but he laughed at himself first. Remember our jester: He comes out as a clown. He's wearing caps and bells, he's frolicking around. He's often someone who just physically has some characteristics that people want to laugh at. Will Rogers makes himself acceptable as a person who can poke fun at others because he made the first joke at his own expense; "I was put lower than the hogs in the slaughterhouse in the Prince of Wales's assessment of sights of America." Now he's free to make jokes at others; but you should never laugh at anybody before you laugh at yourself, just to kind of tie in our being personal with this idea of the uses of humor in public speaking.

We're now to every rich man reaching a time in his career, he comes to a turning point, he starts giving the money away; and he's heard that about some of the guests tonight, and that's one of the reasons he's here. Now his little punch line, "I want to be here for the psychological moment." That tips off the audience there that anybody who hasn't yet given, he's assuming now that the real reason behind this fancy dinner is so that people will open their wallets as they leave or their checkbooks and leave President Butler with a very healthy contribution to the Columbia fund for new buildings. Now he goes on to the reasons, and I bet this got a laugh even though it's not really funny, it's really true; but it sounds like a joke. These other things have been hyperbole, when he said that Columbia was nothing 20 years ago; hyperbole, overstatement, comic overstatement that President Butler has created 100 buildings and annexed Grant's Tomb; more hyperbole, it's a very common form of humor, just overstating the case. He's gone to so much hyperbole that when you hear President Butler had the genius to go around to the alumni, the graduates, and tell them that if they gave money to Columbia it would help on their income tax and perpetuate their names, I'm sure that got a huge laugh: It's the truth; and yet it's told as if it's a joke, it's in the context of the other hyperbole. He's not making many real jokes here; he's building up his information and his delivery of facts in the body of the speech—which is, in fact, a pretty serious speech in terms of its overall message about America, about education, about wealth—he's building it up into a series of punch lines that grow out of the material itself and his comic genius in structuring it for those moments of laughter.

Then this lovely thing at the end when we get into the coursework:

> There are thirty-two hundred courses [I don't know, that may be true; it sounds like a hyperbole]. You spend your first two years in deciding what course to take, the next two years in finding the building that these courses are given in, and the rest of your life in wishing you had taken another course.

That's lovely, and one thing it does is something we saw in Elizabeth and in many other speakers, and when we get to Saint Paul in the next section of the course we'll hear it again: the importance of thinking in threes. You do it when you are making serious points; here's Will Rogers doing it to build the crescendo for the comedy: The first two years, picking your courses; the second two years, looking for the building; and then finally the rest of your life wishing you had taken another course; a big laugh at the end of the whole thing.

We have here some techniques of comedy—the buildup, the surprise, the incongruity, the hyperbole—all of which are things that Will Rogers is a master of; but please notice, every single laugh that he evokes is making a point, every laugh is helping to focus attention on the real substance of his speech. This difference between poor people and rich people and what rich people mean to American education is a very serious subject, and it's a subject so delicate it probably couldn't be addressed at all except through humor. Will Rogers was the right man for President Butler to invite if he wanted a memorable speech. Most after dinner speeches are imminently forgettable; I'm sure the people who were there in Columbia University's dining hall in 1924 all remembered this for the rest of their lives, even if the jokes were at their expense.

I like humor that grows out of the subject you're talking about. I often am talking about history. I found that there was one historical anecdote about the Oracle at Delphi in Greece that when I told it always got a laugh, as if it were that big payoff that people had been waiting for as they sat solemnly and patiently through my description of the archaeological work at Delphi and studying the geological setting of the Oracle. Here's the story, and it helps that it's about someone that they know from history; it's about young Alexander the Great:

> Alexander the Great came to Delphi looking for an Oracle. He was a very young man, he had not yet set out on his campaigns to conquer the world; he wanted a sign from the god Apollo—the god behind the Oracle—speaking through the mouth of the woman who channeled the God's voice (she was the Oracle), he wanted a sign that he was on the right track, that the gods were with him. He got that sign when he went to Delphi. He came on a day when the Oracle was nominally closed. The Oracle was only open for one of the full trance sessions, where the woman would channel the voice of the god in the crypt of the temple one day a month, and only nine months of the year. He didn't come on one of those days, but he's Alexander the Great; and even though he was only in his teens, he wasn't about to be balked of his purpose by tradition or custom at this temple. He went around the village of Delphi, he found the woman, he got her to the temple, and was pushing her down the ramp toward the crypt when she turned to him and said, "Boy, there's no resisting you." Alexander took his hands off her and stepped back and said, "That's the only oracle I wanted to hear." He left, very satisfied with the oracle he got at Delphi.

It takes the audience a minute to understand as they go back to what the Pythia—the woman who gave the oracle—said to Alexander: that he was interpreting her words as if they were the oracle from the god, and not in the temporary meaning of, "Keep roughly handling me; I can't fight you, I can't oppose you, but I don't want to be doing this"; no, he took "There's no resisting you" as the god's word "You will conquer wherever you go." That was almost the truth for his career, so there's then a laugh that comes both with the wits of Alexander in making this play on words and shifting from the sort of petulant teenager to the man who is treating this as the word of a god; many different elements combine to make that a humorous moment, something that I always put in. When I feel that laughter go through the room, I feel people are focused again; and it's not because I told a joke that distracted from the matter at hand, but because I turned something that was central to the whole issue into a source of laughter.

You may wonder: Does every subject lend itself to jokes, or at least to laughter and humor? We need to face the fact in our society that our ideas about solemnity and absence of laughter from great religious occasions or formal occasions is something not shared by the rest of the world. The Greeks were often ready to have laughter at their most sacred moments; they had a god named Dionysius who patronized the comic theater. Sioux Indians out on the American Plains, at their most solemn ceremony, the Sun Dance—which involved bringing dozens of tribes together in a gigantic temporary community with a great lodge in the middle for the ordeal of the Sun Dance—would be awakened every morning of their ceremony, which went on for days, by a sort of crier, a bit of a jester, who would spend his time going through the camp and finding out funny stories and humorous anecdotes about the people who were there. He would ride around the perimeter on a horse at dawn, both being the alarm clock to wake everybody up and at the top of his voice proclaiming these humorous anecdotes about the people who were there. When they were asked about this, the Sioux said, "Laughter opens the spirit to higher things." We don't have that view in our religion in general; laughter is felt to be inappropriate in a solemn occasion, a religious occasion, a mystical occasion. Others have not felt that way; so I think we need to look to other traditions and see how gently they sometimes insert humor into some very serious moments indeed.

I'd like to turn to a speech by a very important fighter, in a metaphorical sense, for rights. She is Burmese; her name is Daw Aung San Suu Kyi, and having won the Nobel Peace Prize in 1991, in 1995 delivered the keynote address to the NGO Forum on Women in Beijing. She wasn't there, she was afraid to leave her native Burma; so she sent her speech on a videotape, and the hundreds of people in attendance crowded in to listen to what she had to say. Her message was extremely serious: The world is in crisis. In half the world, the women are still, in traditional societies, kept from contributing and they're at the mercy of conflicts and wars that are created predominantly by men. Into this extremely serious discourse, she put a couple of very mild jokes. Let me give you the first one; she quotes a Burmese proverb: "The dawn rises only when the rooster crows." You have to take a moment—as I'm sure Will Rogers's audience took a moment sometimes—but then you realize there's a double level here of humor: Silly rooster, so blind that he thinks it is his crowing that brings up the sun. But then you get: Oh, this is about women, women's rights; the rooster is a male, we're seeing a masculine, a male, take on the world, attributing everything, every great important thing, to men. I'm sure there was sort of a two-tiered laugh at that, and also the laugh that comes from surprise, not expecting her to make a joke. She goes on quite seriously to point the moral of this:

> "The dawn rises only when the rooster crows [says the proverb]." But Burmese people today are well aware of the scientific reasons behind the rising of dawn and the falling of dusk. And the intelligent rooster [another jokc] surely realizes that it is because dawn comes that it crows and not the other way round. … It is not the prerogative of men alone to bring light to the world.

By that grand spiritual term "light to the world"—invoking the Buddhist faith, Christian faith, Islam, all of these great religions—she makes that transition from her humor that got us open and laughing and feeling surprised that we could be amused in this way by her speech to the grandest levels of thought and inspiration.

She's going to give another one in her speech; she's prepared us by giving us a little joke at the beginning. Here, toward the end:

> There is an age-old prejudice the world over to the effect that women talk too much [if that did not get a laugh in Beijing, I would be very much surprised]. But is this really a weakness? [She's serious again.] … Women have a most valuable contribution to

make in situations of conflict, by leading the way to solutions based on dialogue.

She took the joking little phrase "women talk too much," kind of turned it on its head—women engage in dialogue where men engage in violence and in action—and drew a message from it. These, to me, are models of what we should pattern our own discourse on when we are giving a public speech and we try to work humor into what we are saying. Remember our Mark Twain, his talk about all the fear that he had as a public speaker for the first time, the knees knocking, his exaggerations of this and that? Remember how he is making a serious message too—nothing is more frightening than stage fright; nothing is more desperate for people who must get up and speak in public—and he is trying to help those who are going to speak in public get around that fear.

Alright, back to my joke: our policeman, our man on the sidewalk, this strange claim, "I'm looking here because the light's better." Notice I didn't tell the joke again; one danger of telling jokes is when you repeat them exactly, people don't want to hear them a second time. Here's the moral: We in archaeology look where the light is good, places like Olduvai Gorge in Africa where we have two millions of years of fossil data exposed by the chance that a river ran through. Is it statistically likely that where the light is good is where the important things happened in human history? No it is not; we are always going to need to be prepared for new revelations in places where the light is currently bad and the darkness is probably concealing the most important clues to early human history.

Let's wrap all this up by turning to some of the lessons that we've learned from Will Rogers and our other speakers today: First, laugh at yourself before you laugh at others. Second, comedy helps relax your audience, especially at formal occasions (remember that Columbia dinner). Third, use humor to focus on your theme, not to distract from it. Fourth, jokes can illuminate serious points, providing new thoughts and perspectives. Fifth, as with every other element of your speech, your humor should reflect your own personality. You may be a person who doesn't like to make jokes, doesn't like to laugh; avoid them, or find the kind of deadpan humor, then, that you need, but make the jokes grow out of yourself as well as from your message. Finally, sixth, nothing unifies an audience quicker than laughter. I find I have a mystical moment when I'm giving lectures when suddenly—and sometimes to my surprise, I'm not aware of having been funny—the whole hall will laugh together, and I feel a little circle of unity, like light, come out from behind me and go around to the back of the hall and click, and I feel we're together. Humor may not come naturally to you, jokes may initially seem artificial and applied from without, but try them; try that additional step toward reaching your audience, because once you hear that laughter, you will know that for the rest of the time, they are with you.

Make It a Story—Marie Curie on Discovery
Lecture 5

I like the word "compose" because it literally means "put together"; it's also something we use for music—that's how composers create their works—and we're going to do it in the same way. Just as they use blocks, tunes, movements, we're going to begin by thinking of ways to put your speech together on a large scale with large building blocks, and then get down to the smaller parts, the individual word choices and so on.

Now we embark on the second phase of our course: We are going to roll up our sleeves, settle down to work, and compose that speech. The speech has two components: It has the substance of the speech, and it has the organization or the manner of presenting it to your audience. The substance of the speech involves coming up with ideas, coming up with facts (you're not literally inventing the facts; that is never a good idea): using your powers of invention to create a mass of facts, of details, of impressions, of narratives, of all kinds of things that you want to convey to your audience. What is it that gives them form and organization? Deciding what comes one after another in the course of your speech. You can give the illusion of three dimensions in your speech; it doesn't have to be a linear story. If you have your opening and then your body of your speech and your conclusion, and in those you tuck in digressions or refer back to things you talked about earlier, you begin to create the sense of three dimensions.

I've always felt that something that is relegated to a minor part of most textbooks on public speaking and rhetoric is the most important thing: storytelling. I believe that the human brain was designed to remember stories; it was not designed to remember facts. But you can make facts memorable by attaching them to stories, to narratives—the same kinds of things that you had read to you as a child. Those stories held your attention because something was happening to a protagonist, and you wanted to know how it ended. If you want to write the most successful speeches, you will find the stories in your subject matter. Pull out those stories, arrange the details and the information that you're trying to get across into the story. Believe me, if you do that, you will not only find it easier to remember your speech, but the audience will also stay with you more closely, pay more attention, understand it better, react with greater grief or laughter or interest, and remember it better.

Let's look at someone who I think is a remarkable example of this: Marie Curie, the famous discoverer of radium and two-time Nobel Prize winner. She was asked to give a graduation speech at Vassar College. She almost never gave public speeches; she was very modest and somewhat shy. How did she approach it? She decided to tell a story. What the people at Vassar were hoping she would do—being this eminent world-famous scientist and a great example of a woman who had broken through all kinds of barriers in terms of acceptance in the scientific community—was to inspire the graduating class of 1921.

By making it a story, Marie Curie made her journey of scientific discovery accessible to a lay audience.

She wanted to tell them all about radium. It's a complicated subject, and she knew that not many of the young women were scientists like herself—how did she go about making it memorable? Let's plunge right in and see:

> Radium is no more a baby, it is more than 20 years old, but the conditions of the discovery were somewhat peculiar, and so it is always of interest to remember them and to explain them.

Look at what she does right from the start: "Radium is no more a baby"; she's almost like a mother talking about her child. She also personifies radium so you feel radium has adventures; radium comes of age, 20 years old. You won't stop of thinking of radium now as the protagonist of this little piece that she's going to tell, this story.

I've always felt that something that is relegated to a minor part of most textbooks on public speaking and rhetoric is the most important thing: storytelling.

She's going to tell the story of how radium was discovered. This will not be an encyclopedia-entry-style, reasoned presentation of what's most important about radium; she's going to tell it as a narrative: how she and her husband began, how they got into it. She is arranging this as a process of discovery: We may not be going with her in terms of knowing and understanding exactly each point, but we understand we're on a journey with her. Skipping ahead a bit:

> But then the activity was not what I would expect.

This is a great narrative device: surprise, wonderment, not what you thought was going to happen.

> And I wanted to find and to separate that element.

We obviously have two protagonists here: She is the questing intelligence, she is the hero in search of that lost treasure; and this unknown element that is out there—radium, although introduced at the beginning, is still not understood to exist by her at this point in the story—that's what she's going after.

This is a great speech; this is a speech that allows everybody in the audience to feel they went on a journey with that discoverer, and that at the end they're standing with her on the mountaintop that she has scaled, looking at the way that she came, and being urged by her to find their own mountains and to climb them in their turn. She has not used colorful language—she was obviously not a practiced public speaker or storyteller—but she had that instinct to take the important points, arrange them as they came up like bubbles from the deep of an unknown thing, and then share the excitement of the discovery and the hard facts of the discovery. She is a scientist; she wants to teach her audience.

If you will do this, if you will seek out the narrative, you will find, first of all, that your speech stays in your mind more clearly; second, that your audience will be with you, and because you're telling a story you'll spend more time looking straight into their eyes and keeping them with you; and third, that when the event is over, years later, after you may have forgotten the occasion and the speech, you will be met by people who thank you for telling that story and let you know how much it's meant to them. ■

Take-Away Points

1. Use stories and narratives to make your speech easy to follow and the details easy to understand and remember.

2. Clearly identify your theme at the beginning of your speech.

3. Include vivid and memorable details that bring your subject to life.

4. Anticipate your audience's questions, and provide the answers in the body of your speech.

Make It a Story—Marie Curie on Discovery

Lecture 5—Transcript

Welcome back. This is the lecture in which we embark on the second phase of our course on "The Art of Public Speaking." We are going to roll up our sleeves, settle down to work, and compose that speech. I like the word "compose" because it literally means "put together"; it's also something we use for music—that's how composers create their works—and we're going to do it in the same way. Just as they use blocks, tunes, movements, we're going to begin by thinking of ways to put your speech together on a large scale with large building blocks, and then get down to the smaller parts, the individual word choices and so on.

I want to throw a few terms at you at this point as sort of part of a roadmap or development through this field of the art of public speaking, some Latin words that have been used since the time of Cicero to describe the different elements of orations and rhetorical pieces. First of all, what have we been doing so far in our first four lectures together? We've been talking about three of Cicero's five elements, or "canons" as he called them, of public speaking. First, we had *elocutio*. Do you remember that pebble in the mouth for Demosthenes? That was the simple production of the text in verbal, in oral form; that's *elocutio*. Second, we went beyond *elocutio* to *pronuntiatio*—or sometimes it was called *actio*, "action"—that was Demosthenes's rule, shared and passed on and exemplified by Patrick Henry, of acting out your speech with your voice, with your body; all the things you do to deliver the speech. *Elocutio*, the words; and then *pronuntiatio*, the delivery of the speech. Then *memoria*, which is "memory." Mark Twain exemplified that for us in his very first public speech when he was so nervous there in San Francisco. He took his script, it was all written down, he tucked it under the American flag, but he found he was able to extemporize by remembering what was on that paper; that is the goal we're trying to reach: the freedom that you have to move about the platform because you're not tied to the podium and look the audience in the eye. *Memoria*, *elocutio*, and then *pronuntiatio*; those are the things we've covered so far.

What are we turning to now as we begin to move toward composing the speech itself? The speech has two components: It has the substance of the speech, and it has the organization or the manner of presenting it to your audience. The substance of the speech comes under Cicero's heading *inventio*, "the invention"; you're coming up with ideas, you're coming up with facts—you're not literally inventing the facts, that is never a good idea—but you are using your powers of invention to create a mass of facts, of details, of impressions, of narratives, of all kinds of things that you want to convey to your audience. What is it that gives them form and organization? *Dispositio*—"disposition" would be the English word—that is how you decide what comes one after another in the course of your speech. You can give the illusion of three dimensions in your speech; it doesn't have to be a linear story. If you start and you have your opening and then your body of your speech and your conclusion, and in those you tuck in digressions or refer back to things you talked about earlier you begin to create the sense of three dimensions; all of this is part of your *dispositio*, and we're going to be talking about that and the *inventio* in these four lectures that make up the second part of our course, "Crafting Your Speech."

I've always felt that something that is relegated to a minor part of most textbooks on public speaking and rhetoric is the most important thing: storytelling. I believe—this is a credo with me—that the human brain was designed to remember stories; it was not designed to remember facts. But you can make facts memorable by attaching them to stories, to narratives; the same kind of things that you had read to you as a child, that held your attention, because something was happening to a protagonist—some adventure, some crisis—you wanted to know how it ended. If you want to write the most successful speeches, you will find ways to find the stories in your subject matter, in that mass of stuff that your *inventio* has pulled together. Pull out those stories, arrange the details and the different facts and the information that you're trying to get across into the story. Believe me, if you do that, you will not only find it easier to remember your speech, but the audience will stay with you more closely, pay more attention, understand it better, react more extremely with greater grief or laughter or interest, and finally after they leave the hall they will remember it better if it was told as a story. That's our focus now, this time: make it a story; use narrative in order to organize your speech and to present it to your audience.

We're going to start with someone who I think is a remarkable example of this; and remember we haven't had many so far. I don't think many public speakers do approach this work of creating the *dispositio*, the organizing element, in terms of a story. As I said, you'll see that reflected in the textbooks where it's often limited to just anecdotes; decorate your speech with little stories, little examples, little anecdotes. I'm going way beyond that: I'm saying find a way to make the whole speech one narrative, one story. Marie Curie, the famous discoverer of radium and two-time Nobel Prize winner, is our guest professor this time. She did a remarkable thing: She was asked to give a graduation speech at Vassar. She almost never gave public speeches; she was very modest and somewhat shy. How did she approach it? She decided to tell a story. What the people at Vassar were hoping she would do—being this eminent world-famous scientist and a great example of a woman who had broken through all kinds of barriers in terms of acceptance in the scientific community—they wanted her to somehow inspire the graduating class of 1921 at Vassar College.

They didn't know how she was going to go about it; and frankly, she was such a giant at that time that almost anything she had said would have made it memorable for those students and their families to think, "I was there in the hall when Marie Curie spoke." She took it more seriously than that. She wanted to tell them all about radium; it's a complicated subject, she knew that not many of the young women were scientists like herself—she wished there were more—how did she go about making it memorable? Let's plunge right in and see:

> Radium is no more a baby, it is more than twenty years old, but the conditions of the discovery were somewhat peculiar, and so it is always of interest to remember them and to explain them.

That's a beautiful beginning; it comes actually after her formal beginning, I've cut into where she starts the substance of her speech. Look at what she does right from the start: Radium is a formidable subject. It's a newly discovered element, it's radioactive, it's already been discovered by 1921 that you can treat cancer with this radium; people know it's important, costly. But all these facts are the kind of things you'd find in an encyclopedia article; how does Marie Curie, the discoverer of radium begin? "Radium is no more a baby"; she's almost like a mother talking about her child. She also personifies radium so you feel radium has adventures; radium comes of age, 20 years old. You're never going to forget the fact that radium was 20 years old when she gave the speech; you won't stop of thinking of radium now as the protagonist of this little piece that she's going to tell, this story.

I think it's also important that Marie Curie wants to give you her personal feelings; look at how much of herself is in this first sentence: "the conditions of the discovery were somewhat peculiar"; that is a subjective opinion that only she could have (she and her husband, who was her partner in working on this). "Somewhat peculiar," that's not a scientific term, that's the kind of term that anybody in the hall could use about a puzzle; something that raises a question, a sort of a whodunit and "how did it get done" kind of mystery, and it's getting your audience to want to know the solution to a puzzle, or the ending to a story (a cliffhanger), that's what's going to keep them focused on your words. Then I really like her giving you the image of herself and her husband with memory: "it is always of interest to remember them"; that they sit around and look back on this and they want to share that with you, and to explain them.

She's picked the right way to explain them: She's going to tell the story of how radium was discovered. This will not be an encyclopedia-entry-style, reasoned presentation of what's most important about radium, somewhat less important, and least important details; she's going to tell it as a narrative: how they began, how they got into it. I'm not saying that everything in this will be crystal clear to us—you could hardly pick a more formidable subject—but let's see how she does it:

> We must go back to the year 1897. [This is Marie Curie's version of "Once upon a time."] Professor Curie and I worked at that time in the laboratory of the school of Physics and Chemistry. I was engaged in some work on uranium rays which had been discovered two years before … I spent some time in studying the way of making good measurements of the uranium rays, and then I wanted to know if there were other elements giving out rays of the same kind. So I took up a work about all known elements and their compounds …

> I found that several of those which contain uranium or thorium or both were active [in other words, radioactive].

She is arranging this as a process of discovery: We may not be going with her in terms of knowing and understanding exactly each point, but we understand we're on a journey with her; the narrative has begun; we're moving from ignorance to understanding, and doing that primeval journey from darkness to light with Marie Curie.

> But then the activity was not what I would expect. …

This is a great narrative device: surprise, wonderment, not what you thought was going to happen.

> Then I thought there should be in the minerals some unknown element, having a greater radioactivity than uranium or thorium.

This is a little example of her slightly unidiomatic English: "then I thought there should be in the minerals" we would say, "then I thought there must be in the minerals"; but I'm sure they had no trouble following her there in the hall at Vassar.

> And I wanted to find and to separate that element …

We obviously have two protagonists here: She is the questing intelligence, she is the hero in search of that lost treasure; and this unknown element that is out there—radium, although introduced at the beginning, is still not understood to exist by her at this point in the story—that's what she's going after.

> We thought it would be done in several weeks or months, but it was not so. It took many years of hard work to finish that task. There was not one new element, there were several of them [element of surprise]. But the most important is radium. … The intensity of its rays are several million times greater than the uranium rays. And the effects of the rays make the radium so important … producing physiological effects on cells of the human organism, for the cure

> of diseases. Most important is the treatment of cancer. From its ore, America produces many grams of radium every year, but the price is still very high because the quantity of radium contained in the ore is so small. Radium is more than a hundred thousand times more precious than gold.

Marie Curie is a little like the late Carl Sagan here with his billions and billions of stars, but she's trying to give her audience a sense, without bothering them with specific numbers they won't be able to remember, of the magnitude of what she's talking about: the high cost of the radium, the million times more radioactive than uranium; all of these things, they're not going to be able to take the scientist aside and explain exactly what degrees or what numbers are involved, but they have a sense, "We're looking at worlds of difference and of magnitude here."

> When radium was discovered, no one knew that it would prove useful in hospitals. The work was one of pure science, which must be done for itself, for the beauty of science. …

If there was one expression I think nobody in that hall would have expected to hear, it was "the beauty of science." This is obviously something very soul-enhancing for her; it raises her spirit; it makes her see things in the universe we don't see as nonscientists or non-hard scientists. She's working up to a message:

> It is my earnest desire that some of you should carry on this scientific work, and keep for your ambition the determination to make a permanent contribution to science.

That is a great speech; that is a speech that allows everybody in the audience to feel they went on a journey with that discoverer, and that at the end they're standing with her on the mountaintop that she has scaled, looking at the way that she came and being urged by her to find their own mountains and to climb them in their turn. She has not used colorful language—she was obviously not a practiced public speaker or storyteller—but she had that instinct to take the important points, arrange them as they sort of came up like bubbles from the deep of an unknown thing, and then share the excitement of the discovery and the hard facts of the discovery. She is a scientist; she wants to teach, she wants to instruct with her audience.

What makes details memorable? What makes details memorable is their importance in a narrative or in a story. I'd like to go from Marie Curie now to another writer, someone in the oral tradition, who we're going to hark back to more than once in this lecture: the poet Homer, the man who created or composed *The Iliad* and *The Odyssey*. Homer likes to describe things, but he likes to describe important things. One of his famous descriptions involves a scar: his hero Odysseus has a scar on his leg. Odysseus can be recognized by that scar; he got it in youth. He's come home to his palace in Ithaca, discovering that his palace has been taken over by enemies—suitors for his wife's hand—because he's been gone so long everybody thinks he's dead. He is powerless as one man to tackle them; he will need to use trickery, he will need to get allies, and he needs to initially get inside the palace, scope out the land, and see what course of action he should take.

His great risk is that he will be recognized; he is recognized as soon as she approaches his palace there on the island of Ithaca. He walks up to the gate. Beside the gate is the manure heap they throw out from the domestic animals and will take out to manure the fields, and lying on that manure heap, pathetically, is an old dog. It's his old dog, last seen years before when the dog was a puppy and he was a young man going off to lead the Ithacans in the war at Troy. The dog recognizes his old master. Odysseus is in beggar's rags; it wags its tail. Odysseus goes through the gate; he daren't recognize the dog or pet it or show that he is the master. He crosses the courtyard and goes inside that building, and he's ultimately welcomed by his wife as a beggar who might bring news of her husband from abroad. The wife, Penelope, tells one of the old maidservants—in fact, Odysseus's own nurse from his boyhood days—"Wash his feet." He turns away quickly from the firelight, remembering the scar; but the old woman grabs the leg before he can stops her, lifts it up to begins to scrub the dust of the journey off the leg, and she sees the scar. She's shocked, and she remembers how he got it: He got it out boar hunting on the slopes of Mount Taladon when he was a young man, joining a group of other heroes. At that moment, the nurse—whose name is Eurycleia—drops the leg. It splashes in the basin of water; Odysseus reaches down and clamps his hand over her mouth so that she won't speak.

Penelope, fortunately, has had her attention distracted and doesn't catch on to what's happening.

You're never going to forget that scar, you're never going to forget that he got it in a boar's hunt because Homer has given it weight in the narrative: It's the detail that could blow Odysseus's cover; could reveal who he truly is; could lead to his death and the ruin of his family and of his palace. That's what makes details vivid: It's not so much the language you pack around them; it's placing them in a spot in your narrative where they are turning points or where they are key things. That then allows your audience to follow the story, to wrap its mind and its memory around those details, and keep them, vividly, in a realistic kind of way in their minds as if it were part of their own experience. That's the highest art for me, or one of the highest arts, that any public speaker can command.

You find story form in lots of the world's literature. It tends to be especially prevalent where cultures had what we call "oral tradition"; in other words, they were more about learning to speak and tell stories and hold people's attention in grand public orations or around fires at night, passing down history as a series of remembered chronicles rather than just pulling a book off the shelf and consulting it. The vivid use of the detail, the assignment to certain objects or images great importance is very common to this oral tradition. I'd like to move now, we've had Homer, let's move to a different kind of oral tradition: that of the Gospels in the Christian Bible, which were originally spoken documents, and look at the story of the Good Samaritan as told by Jesus.

In the Gospel according to Saint Luke, Jesus has just said, "Love your God and love your neighbor as yourself," and a lawyer has asked him, "Who is my neighbor?" A good lawyer's question. Jesus has not yet really defined his terms, and he's said something shocking: that you should love—you should feel this *agape*, this open, tolerant welcome—to somebody you don't even know well, a neighbor; so Jesus tells a story rather than providing a dictionary-style definition and his response is much more powerful because it is a story.

> A certain man went down from Jerusalem to Jericho, and fell among thieves, which stripped him of his raiment, and wounded him, and departed, leaving him for dead. And by chance there came down a certain priest that way: and when he saw him, he passed by on the other side. And likewise a Levite, when he was at the place, came and looked on him, and passed by on the other side. But a certain Samaritan, as he journeyed, came where he was; and when he saw him, he had compassion on him. And went to him, and bound up his wounds, pouring in oil and wine, and set him on his own beast, and brought him to an inn, and took care of him. ... Which now of these three, thinkest thou, was neighbor unto him that fell among the thieves? And he said [the lawyer], He that showed mercy on him. Then said Jesus unto him, Go, and do thou likewise.

Jesus never really answers the question, but he tells this long story; and I submit to you that one of the things that makes the story so powerful is that it's a real story. Let's look at all the little elements that Jesus uses to draw you into this story: First, it's personal; we have a hero, we have this Samaritan. It's not clearly understood by many people in the modern world that for a Jew like Jesus to talk about a Samaritan to another Jew was to talk about a person who was untouchable, a pariah, someone who belonged to a fallen, divorced branch of the old Hebrew people; the northerners who had, according to the Jews of Jerusalem and the area around Jerusalem, gone the wrong way. There should be no discourse with these people; they should not be touched, they should not be helped; you should not even go into their territory. That's who the Samaritan is; and the first two people to pass by are, in fact, Jews. The Samaritan comes and sees the Jew who has been beaten up, who has been left for dead; the Samaritan, our hero, is the one who is the least likely. So Jesus is using that confounding of expectations, that element of surprise: A Jew was beaten up; two Jews went by; a Samaritan is the one who stopped.

If he had just told that story, it's not much of a story; it's Jesus's details that draw you in. what went into the wound to treat it? There was some oil and there was some wine; wine is a disinfectant, the alcohol in it helps wounds. What did the Samaritan do to get the poor victim of this robbery to the inn? He put him on his own beast, his own mule or whatever animal was carrying him. Then the fact that we are told very specifically where the man was going in the first place: This Jew was going down from Jerusalem to Jericho. None of these details really matter because they're not real—this is not a real story Jesus has told from the headlines—but they do matter for holding your attention. The details become vivid, you get more into the story, it becomes real to you and the situation suddenly takes you over; and when Jesus says, "Which one of these three was the man's neighbor?" suddenly there's great weight to that answer. The lawyer won't even say "the Samaritan," he just says "He that had mercy." But that's the point: Jesus has used the story for instruction. His whole answer to that man, that lawyer, was a story; the story carried the message more strongly, more concretely than any possible explicit statement of words.

I've found in my own life and in my own career that telling stories is the way to hold people's interest in the classroom. For a long time, I needed money and I would teach night school; two-and-a-half hours on Tuesdays, two-and-a-half hours on Thursday nights to classrooms of people who had worked all day and who probably had families to go home to. How was I going to keep them interested? At first I tried notes; I was trying to share what was in their textbooks, I was trying to give organized lists of facts, I was trying to be very organized (which is not really very typical of me). It didn't seem to work; I could tell from the way that they were drifting off to sleep, their feet were pointing toward the door in that unmistakable body language sign of "I want to get out of here," or they'd get up and leave. In self-defense, because I didn't want to be a failure at this, I began to tell a few stories; I began to tie the facts in their coursework to anecdotes. I found immediately when I did that the focus was on, the attention was there; people were able to stick with it. I ultimately made those two-and-a-half hour lectures one big narrative with a series of smaller narratives threaded, like beads on a string, inside. I found it easy to remember the sequence; I no longer had to look down at notes or back at a blackboard, I could be with them as we went through this story and series of stories together. That was my own experience as a teacher.

As a coach, I had the same experience that is commemorated in that famous movie involving Ronald Reagan in which there is a locker room speech where the coach is sending the young players out saying, "You know, there was an old team player, his name was the Gipper, and one day he said to me, 'Coach, when they're down and victory seems impossible'—and he told this long, tear-jerking story about this former player—'tell them to win one for the Gipper.' " The story was the point: pulling them in, making them feel strong about it, making them feel that the story had empowered them. That's what stories can do for you if you will find the story in your material and build your speech around it.

Let's look at some of our lessons that we get from Marie Curie, from the Gospels, about how to use stories; we can throw in Homer as well. First of all—and for me this is the key to public speaking; everything else is secondary to this—use stories and narratives to make your speech easy to follow and the details easy to understand and remember. You may have to sweat to find the story within your material, but it's worth the effort. Second, clearly identify your theme at the beginning of your speech. Marie Curie: Radium is no longer a baby; it's 20 years old and I'm going to tell you about its growing up. Or Jesus: The theme was given to him by the question, "Who is my neighbor?" Be sure they understand the point of the story before you launch in or they'll get drowned in the details, they'll get drowned in the twists and turns of your tale. Third, include vivid and memorable details that bring your subject to life. Don't smooth out the story so it becomes abstract; it is the details that will make it memorable. Then, anticipate your audience's questions and provide the answers in the body of your speech; somehow touch on them in the course of that narrative or story. Remember how beautifully that was done both by Marie Curie with her answering all the questions about radium so you really felt you understood most of the details about this very important, newly discovered element; but also in the Gospel story of the Good Samaritan, questions about belonging to a certain religion or belonging to a certain community. The lawyer had not asked that question, but Jesus anticipated it and made sure that his story provided the answers.

If you will do this, if you will seek out the narrative, you will find, first of all, your own speech stays in your mind more clearly; second, that your audience will be with you, and because you're telling a story you'll spend more time looking straight into their eyes and keeping them with you; and third, when the event is over, I guarantee you, years later, after you may have forgotten the occasion and the speech, you will be met by people who thank you for telling that story and let you know how much it's meant to them.

Use the Power of Three—Paul to His People

Lecture 6

If you were told that Winston Churchill once said during World War II that all that he could offer the British people was "blood, sweat, and tears," you would say, "I knew that"; you'd be wrong. What he actually said in that famous speech was "I have nothing to offer you but blood, toil, tears, and sweat"; a foursome. The popular mind could not hold onto that foursome; the "toil" had to go. … Nothing shows me the power of three more strongly than this fact.

In our last lecture, we talked about my belief that it's very important to make your speech, wherever possible, a story; and it's a well-known fact that every story has three parts: a beginning, a middle, and an end. This lecture's continuation is about tripartite structures and presenting things in threes. Just as I believe the human brain was designed to remember stories but not masses of facts, I believe the human mind was also designed to find threes satisfying, and to feel that something presented in threes has made its case. Two of something seems in opposition; three of something seems a completion. There can be threes in terms of three modifiers for a noun, the tripartite story we just talked about, or three phrases or examples. All of these things are tremendously important things to consider as you lay out that speech and begin to organize your material within it.

To get into this world of threes, I want to plunge us all into the oratory of what I think is perhaps the single most inspired piece of prose ever conceived: The famous 13th chapter from the first letter that Paul wrote to the Corinthians. We have to talk first about the word, the subject, of this talk that Paul is giving to us. In Greek, the word is *agape*, just like "agape," or "open." *Agape* means "an open welcome"; it means tolerance, getting along with people, and treating everyone alike.

The Corinthians—this congregation that Paul had helped to start—were quarreling among themselves, and he's writing to them about getting along and what really matters in this world. Here is the conclusion as an example.

Notice how much of this incredible piece of writing is governed by this rule of threes:

> When I was a child, I spake as a child, I understood as a child, I thought as a child: but when I became a man, I put away childish things. For now we see through a glass, darkly; but then face to face; now I know in part; but then I shall know even as also I am known. And now abideth faith, hope, agape, these three: but the greatest of these is agape.

It's often said when people are talking to you about making your speech, your public talk, in a three-part form, that the introduction and the body of the speech and the conclusion play very simple roles. You will sometimes see this sort of mantra: First, tell them what you are going to tell them; second, in the body, tell them; and then, in the conclusion, tell them again what you told them. This seems to me a counsel of despair and desperation; who wants to really hear things three times? Paul doesn't give you things three times; you feel you know where you are at every point in this wonderful sermon, but there's not the kind of repetition that the model implies. I believe in the three-part structure, but I believe those are the wrong things to put in the parts.

Two of something seems in opposition; three of something seems a completion.

What do we have in the first part, the introduction? He has made you curious about *agape*. Instead of telling you what he's going to say about it, he has announced it as the subject of his sermon and he has filled you with wonder and questions and confusion about exactly what it is; how can this rather everyday kind of quality of an open, tolerant welcome be tied up with these men and angels and sounding brasses?

Now we go on to the body of the speech: The body of the speech carries your message. It should be easy to follow; the forms should be clear, the diction, the choice of words, the presentation should all help the person follow your meaning as you go along. Having begun to feel that he's gotten you on board, he's willing to bring back some of the stuff from the introduction to unify the whole speech, thematically and in tone.

Paul's use of tripartite structures heightened his extraordinary imagery.

He finally comes to a conclusion. Please, follow Paul's example and make the conclusion open up, broaden, shed new light, bring in more ideas and more feeling. How does he do that? Suddenly, we're back to our Lecture 3: Be personal; make it about yourself. It has not been so far, but now he signals a change; he brings it home. We're getting a sense of chords being struck again and again, of the thing bounding, and finally that great surprise with things brought in that you haven't even been talking about in this final triad. In fact, I would recommend you never repeat yourself in your conclusion. I think there are few more deadening words than either "To sum up" or "As I said before"; people's minds switch off. The end of your speech should be a climax, not a sinking back to a summary or repetition of what came before. ■

Take-Away Points

1. Construct your speech in three parts: introduction, body, and conclusion.

2. Create a rhythm with clauses, examples, and parallel sentences in groups of three.

3. Use adjectives and other short sequences of words in threes.

Use the Power of Three—Paul to His People

Lecture 6—Transcript

Welcome back. In our last lecture, we talked about my belief that it's very important to make your speech, wherever possible, a story; and it's a well-known fact that every story has three parts: a beginning, a middle, and an end. Today's continuation, as we work on the *dispositio*—the arrangement and organization of the material within your speech—is about tripartite structures and presenting things in threes. Just as I believe the human brain was designed to remember stories but not masses of facts, I believe the human mind was also designed to find threes satisfying, and to feel that something presented in threes has made its case. Two of something seems in opposition; three of something seems a completion. There can be threes in terms of three modifiers for a noun, the tripartite story we just talked about, or three phrases or examples; all of these things are tremendously important things to consider as you lay out that speech and begin to organize your material within it.

In order to get into this world of threes, I want to plunge us all into the oratory of what I think is perhaps the single most inspired piece of prose ever conceived: It's that famous 13th chapter from the first letter that Paul wrote to the Corinthians. It's the section that you've heard so many times at weddings and other occasions; it's usually called a passage on love or on charity, but that's not the word he used. Nonetheless, we're going to talk about the historical background a little, we're going to talk about the word I'm going to use for the subject of this short speech—and I believe it was a sermon and not just a letter—and then we're going to go through it bit by bit.

We have to talk first about the word, the subject, of this talk that Paul is giving to us. In Greek, the word is *agape*, just like "agape," "open"; it's the same word. *Agape* means "an open welcome"; it goes back to Homer, to very ancient, archaic Greek. It means tolerance, it means getting along with people, it means treating everyone alike, it means being friendly and welcoming to all. We don't have such a word in English, this is one of the many ways in which English can fail to adequately represent words in another language; and, of course, no two languages are completely consistent in how they choose their vocabularies to describe the world. Although "love" has been chosen by most of the modern translations of the Gospels as the subject of

Paul's speech or letter, and although the King James Version chose "charity," "charity" sounds too much like a handout (that's not what it's about) and "love" sounds too warm, rich, specifically emotional—How am I supposed to love my neighbor as myself or as my parents or as my children or spouse or beloved one?—and yet it's also tied in with just trivial things: loving ice cream, loving the Fourth of July (not that the Fourth of July is trivial).

At any rate, let's just use the Greek term; let's get into Paul's letter. The Corinthians were quarreling among themselves—this congregation that he had helped to start—and he's writing to them about getting along and what really matters in this world. Here we go; I'm going to give you the three parts of the speech as we go. The introduction is, of course, the beginning, in which he sets up the subject of this talk, this letter, this sermon. Then we have the body of the speech where almost every sentence begins with the word, *agape*; that open, tolerant, welcome, and acceptance of all. Then, when we get to "When I was a child, I spake as a child," we're into the conclusion; it suddenly shifts to a personal statement, we feel we're on new ground, and he wraps it all up with a little narration about the child growing up, becoming a man, and now seeing things as they really are. Notice how much of this incredible piece of writing is governed by this rule of threes:

> Thou I speak with the tongues of men and of angels, and have not agape, I am become as sounding brass, or a tinkling cymbal. And though I have the gift of prophecy, and understand all mysteries, and all knowledge; and though I have all faith, so that I could remove mountains, and have not agape, I am nothing. And though I bestow all my goods to feed the poor, and though I give my body to be burned, and have not agape, it profiteth me nothing.
>
> Agape suffereth long, and is kind; agape envieth not; agape vaunteth not itself, is not puffed up, doth not behave itself unseemly, seeketh not her own, is not easily provoked, thinketh no evil, rejoiceth not in iniquity, but rejoiceth in truth; beareth all things, believeth all things, hopeth all things, endureth all things. Agape never faileth: but where there be prophecies, they shall fail; where there be tongues, they shall cease; where there be knowledge it shall vanish away. For we know in part, and we prophesy in part, but when

> that which is perfect is come, then that which is in part shall be done away.
>
> When I was a child, I spake as a child, I understood as a child, I thought as a child: but when I became a man, I put away childish things. For now we see through a glass, darkly; but then face to face; now I know in part; but then I shall know even as also I am known. And now abideth faith, hope, agape, these three: but the greatest of these is agape.

It's an extraordinary passage, but part of its effect is its structure; that skeleton, that mass of bones and tissue behind the words, that make Paul's meaning so powerful and make us feel we have come on a progression with him, a story, a journey. We've started in the introduction with visions: speaking with the tongues of men and of angels, sounding brasses, tinkling cymbals, the gift of prophesy, mysteries, all knowledge, all faith, moving mountains. Then extravagant things: bestowing goods on the poor, giving your body to be burned. That's our introduction; extraordinary set of images, vivid—that word that means "lively," "living" that I'm always urging that you try to find in your images—Paul really does that.

It's often said when people are talking to you about making your speech, your public talk, in a three-part form, that the introduction and the body of the speech and the conclusion play very simple roles. You will sometimes see this sort of mantra: First, tell them what you are going to tell them; second, in the body, tell them; and then, in the conclusion, tell them again what you told them (obviously in a summary form at the beginning and the end, and with all of the material in the middle). This seems to me a counsel of despair and desperation; who wants to really hear things three times? Paul doesn't give you things three times; you feel you know where you are at every point in this wonderful sermon, but there's not the kind of repetition that the model implies. I believe in the three-part structure, but I believe those are the wrong things to put in the parts.

What do we have in the first part, the introduction? He has made you curious about *agape*. Instead of telling you what he's going to say about it, he has announced it as the subject of his sermon and he has filled you with wonder and questions and confusion about exactly what it is; how can this rather everyday kind of quality of an open, tolerant welcome be tied up with these men and angels and sounding brasses? He's going to tell us in the middle; but you see what that first part did, that introduction: It gave you the subject of the talk; you are in no doubt about that, that this is going to be about this quintessential character, this *agape*, this feeling of openness that in the very last line is going to be introduced as the greatest thing in the world, the most abiding thing. There's faith, there's hope, there's charity; *agape*, charity, love: that is the supreme one. That's where we're going: He's not going to tell you that at the beginning, he's just going to give you these clouds of visions. Part of the point of an introduction—after that first element that is explain or introduce the subject—is arouse curiosity, wonder, a desire to know more; and boy does he succeed in that with these wild images about this still somewhat mysterious characteristic, *agape*.

Now we go on to the body of the speech: The body of the speech carries your message. When I'm trying to put together a lecture, all the things I think will be—as we say—on the test go into the body of the speech. If a lawyer is giving a summing up, the opening may introduce the problem, arouse the jury's emotions, and so on but the middle, the body, needs to present in a coherent fashion and a compelling way—maybe as a narrative, maybe in some other form—everything the listener needs to know to feel they understand the meaning and make an informed opinion about it themselves. Let's see how Paul does it: "Agape suffereth long," he says at the very start of his body of the speech, "is kind; agape envieth not." This is the way you define things in a dictionary; he wants to make the subject of the speech, what it is? He wants to give you all these characteristics of it; and the body of the speech is very coherent, very straightforward. He's explaining to you a great mystery—that this characteristic of being open to all people should be all these different things—but he's presenting it to you like a textbook.

I think here we can see why it would be inappropriate for him to speak in parables. He is assigning to *agape* a mystical belief—it is that thing out of the parable of the Good Samaritan that we saw last time that made that Samaritan stop; that was *agape*—but he's wanting to get at it crisply; he's wanting to get at it not mysteriously at first, but in a sort of a very regular, almost scientific, descriptive way. The body of your speech should be like that: It should be easy to follow; the forms should be clear, the diction, the choice of words, the presentation should all help the person follow your meaning as you go along.

Then, having begun to feel that he's gotten you on board, he's willing to bring back some of the stuff from the introduction to unify the whole speech, thematically and in tone (the tone of grandeur, the tone of prophecy): "Agape never faileth." We think we're in for more of the sort of "it is this, it is that," but no: "but where there be prophecies, they shall fail; where there be tongues, they shall cease; where there be knowledge it shall vanish away." You notice his threes there; he's continuing to use those triads, that rhythm; he's a preacher. I'm descended in the third generation from a Baptist preacher and I certainly feel that rhythm when it comes, I feel swept up by it. He's starting to want to get beyond the definitions and get into the emotion again that he stirred up in his introduction with all those extraordinary images. Then we get into this question of knowledge: "For we know in part, and we prophesy in part, but when that which is perfect is come, then that which is in part shall be done away." The words are simple, the meaning is obscure; but that's how it all wraps up. What we can know in this world is that this *agape* is the most important thing.

Having presented that in the body of his speech, he finally comes to a conclusion: If we were to take that rule of tell them what you're going to tell them (that's the introduction), tell them (that's the body), tell them what you told them (that's the conclusion), you would have hammered away at it enough perhaps that it might be remembered, but please, follow Paul's example and follow the example of all other good speech composers in giving people something new and making the conclusion open up, broaden, shed new light, bring in more ideas and more feeling. Let's see how he does that. Suddenly, we're back to our Lecture 3: be personal; make it about yourself. It has not been so far, but now listen what he does to signal the change to the conclusion; he brings it home: "When I was a child, I spake as a child, I understood as a child, I thought as a child"—his triad again—"but when I became a man, I put away childish things." One of those childish things is not understanding the world; his eyes are being opened with maturity. "For now we see through a glass, darkly"; mirrors and windows in the Roman world that Paul lived in were not the clear glass we have today. "But then"—

that is, in the future, when we are truly grown up—we shall see "face to face; now I know in part; but then I shall know even as also I am known."

Knowledge is what this is about; knowing what matters in the world. He introduced a motif—as we might say in music—of knowledge in the first part, in the introduction; he's giving you the knowledge in the second part, the body; and now he's referring to it at the end to close it all off. We're getting a sense of chords being struck again and again, of the thing bound together by motifs that keep you focused on the meaning, and finally that great surprise with things brought in that you haven't even been talking about in this final triad. "And now abideth faith, hope, agape, these three: but the greatest of these is agape"; a perfect climax. He's giving you one more fact about this remarkable quality that he is urging you to prize in your life, and to seek, and to recognize as the most important thing in this world, and he's listing these gigantic qualities—faith, hope—no, *agape* is greater than any of them. Then he stops; and it's very important as you're crafting your speech that when you have covered in your introduction the essential elements of explaining the subject, rousing curiosity about it, and setting the tone of the speech—those three things—and then in the body of the speech, giving them all the information they need to know; applying this to them, to their world; and finally, building up a vivid picture through images that allows them to apply this beyond the confines of your speech, apply it to their lives; he does that throughout the body of his speech here. When you get to the conclusion, you are free then to add new elements; to raise the ante, as we would say in poker; to make things even higher, more dramatic, more strong, more forceful and emotional through some new elements. Don't feel tied to just repeating yourself in your conclusion; in fact, I would recommend you never repeat yourself in your conclusion. I think there are few more deadening words than either "To sum up" or "As I said before"; people's minds switch off. The end of your speech should be a climax, not a sinking back to a summary or repetition of what came before.

We can go way beyond Saint Paul in finding threes; you find them almost everywhere. Let me give you a couple that we haven't heard from before, and then we're going to go back and look at our former guest professors and see how often they also follow Paul in this idea of the triad as an essential building block as you put together your speech. Here we go: Sir Winston

Churchill—this one is fascinating to me—if you were told that Winston Churchill once said during World War II that all that he could offer the British people was "blood, sweat and tears," you would say, "I knew that"; you'd be wrong. What he actually said in that famous speech was "I have nothing to offer you but blood, toil, tears and sweat"; a foursome. The popular mind could not hold onto that foursome; the "toil" had to go. I don't think it's because they're lazy and didn't want to work hard, I think it's because four is too many; and nothing shows me the power of three more strongly than this fact that popular consciousness took Winston Churchill's "blood, toil, tears and sweat," something that was printed from the day that he spoke it and distributed widely, and yet turned it simply by activity of the popular mind and memory into the unforgettable "blood, sweat and tears."

Let's stay in England for a moment and go to an occasion that many of us can remember: the funeral of Princess Diana, Princess of Wales. Her brother, Charles, Earl of Spencer, spoke the eulogy; that was in 1997. He uses all the way through this eulogy some of these techniques of using the triad. The eulogy, of course, does have its introduction, its middle, its conclusion; and, like, Paul, he brings in new things in the conclusion—reflections on the sons and what will be their future—that keep a sense of movement in the speech, that keep a sense of new things opening up, even though you do feel him coming to a conclusion. We're not going to have the whole speech; let me just give you a couple of examples of his triads. This is the very beginning of his eulogy, spoken in Westminster Abbey:

> I stand before you today the representative of a family in grief, in a country in mourning, before a world in shock …

It's a very strong opening; it's a very rhetorical opening. He has decided to save his strong emotional effects and his personal comments and revelations for later on in the eulogy so he has somewhere to go emotionally. In fact, by using the triad he creates a sort of feeling of objectivity about it; this is the way you look at the world and assess: What is the death of this young woman mean in the widening circles of geography, of family, of country, of the world? That gives him room to move as he gets on into the body of the eulogy. Later on, he's talking to her; he's addressing her directly—her memory, Diana—and he's opposing those who want to turn her into a saint:

> To sanctify your memory would be to miss out on the very core of your being: your wonderfully mischievous sense of humor; your joy for life; your boundless energy which you could scarcely contain.

There's something very satisfying about that, has he knew there would be. One feels like a character has been described, that enough facets have been presented that we feel we knew this woman; and that's what he's after.

Musical form is a good guide for us here, as is the form that novels take. Always be thinking, as you put together your speech, of stories, books that you've read, think how the opening chapters of any novel are presenting to you the characters, the situation (the place), and the themes—the important sense of what's going to happen, what is the basic underlying story, it all comes in that introduction—and you also get the tone; and that's something the Earl of Spencer in this eulogy has tried to do, Saint Paul also: Saint Paul, a tone of exaltation and almost mysticism; the Earl of Spencer a sense that "I am talking about something that matters to the world." That's what he wants you to get right away: This is a big, momentous occasion. All that comes in the first chapters of a novel, the beginning; then, in the middle—the body of it—comes the working out. If we were talking in musical terms, we'd say the opening of the novel is the exposition where all the themes are laid out by the composer. The middle of the novel, which usually contains the strife, the conflicts, all of the surprises—if we're headed for a happy ending, we're sure not going to be happy in the middle, because we need somewhere to go to with the resolution—that would be the middle of your speech; that's where you're putting all of your ideas in play and watching them sort of thrash it out, dealing with the difficult problems. Then we finally get, in music, to the recapitulation; we get back to the themes of the beginning, now in a proper order and tonality. In a novel, we get to that concluding part of the novel, which often is quite short, in which all the problems are resolved; where the tone, if it was tragic, has carried things through to their horrible, logical conclusion, or if it was comic or optimistic has resolved all of the difficulties from the middle part of the novel and given you a satisfying ending. Three parts; remember to put those into your speech and you will have that same successful outcome that a good novel has and the same wonderful impact on your listeners that a good novelist is able to have on the reader.

Let's just review some of this as we look back at some of our previous speakers to see how universal this is. I know I'm beating this like a dead horse; but that, of course, is onomatopoeia in a way for what the power of three does: You keep hammering away at the thing, and after three blows people get it. Here we are, for instance, back with Will Rogers. I'm sure it wasn't some sort of very bookish kind of thought and objective analysis that made him talk in threes, but here's a nice ending to his speech as he talks about the classes, the array of classes at Columbia:

> There are thirty-two hundred courses. You spend your first two years in deciding what course to take, the next two years in finding the building that these courses are given in, and the rest of your life in wishing you had taken another course.

That's a very humorous passage, but it builds very satisfyingly; it seems rounded off by the third one, but you come up three steps. He has intensified, as well as rounded off, something you can do very effectively with three; you can't do it with twos, and as soon as you get more than three—maybe it's just something about what the human brain can normally take in through its years—you begin to lose track of what's being considered.

Let's go to England and to Elizabeth I, talking to her men at Tilbury: "I myself will be your general, judge, and rewarder of every one of your virtues in the field." She could have added 15 other things she is to them; she knew 3 is the right number. At the end, she repeats a triad, a threesome that she introduced earlier: "By your valour in the field, we shall shortly have a famous victory over those enemies of my God, of my kingdom, and of my people." Here, we can see a difference between her and Will Rogers: Will Rogers has varied his threesome. "You spend the first two years" in this, "you spend your next two years" in this; you expect "you spend your last two years." He has expanded it, he's given a sense of opening up, by making his ending "and the rest of your life in wishing"; and that's part of the hyperbole that makes it funny. She is trying for a very tight parallelism; her clauses are parallel, they all begin with "of": "of my God," "of my kingdom," and "of my people." That will give you a more consistent set of words that will help you put your threesomes into a more consistent arrangement and give them more impact for your listener.

Let's go on to Sojourner Truth; she has one phrase where she does the same thing that Elizabeth just did: "We do as much, we eat as much, we want as much." (The "we" is women.) But see how powerful that is, like the ringing of a bell, when her clauses are exactly parallel to each other, each one beginning with "we" and then the verb, and ending with "as much." You could not have a more forceful use of threes and the parallelisms of threes. She began, also, the passage that we began with: "I have been forty years a slave and forty years free, and would be here forty years more to have equal rights for all." The forty/forty/forty; it's the backbone of the expression. Is it really tied into the meaning? What does that have to say about her desire for women's rights? That's not so clear; but you are riveted by that, and you remember those figures, and you feel that you have been carried along, you've moved with her, through that progression that she is so careful in evoking.

Finally, let's look at our example of the Good Samaritan, that story. Jesus, you will remember, in describing his story that explains "who is your neighbor" has decided to have three characters walk by the man who has been robbed, beaten, and left for dead on the road between Jerusalem and Jericho; three men. Why three? If you look at the world's folklore, you will see time and again three tasks, three brothers, three talismans, three achievements; universal folk consciousness moves in threes. Jesus has used that expectation so that when we see three come along and two fail the test—pass by on the other side—we are ready with a sense of completion and a sense of rightness when that third one stops and helps.

Our lessons this time are three in number, and they're brief, and they're simple, just as the triad form tends to be. First, construct your speech in three parts: introduction, body, and conclusion. Second, create a rhythm with clauses, examples, and parallel sentences in groups of three. Finally, getting even down to the molecular structure of your speech, use adjectives and other short sequences of words in threes. It's not so important in written language, in creating books or articles, but believe me: When you are up in front of a crowd and you want to hold their interest, make your meaning clear, and create a sense of order and form in your speech, you should always remember the power of three.

Build a Logical Case—Susan B. Anthony

Lecture 7

I believe if you can learn from our great guest professors, if you can take to heart what they show you about the step-by-step progression of building a logical speech, your logic will be able to prevail in almost any argument that you choose to make.

In this lecture, we consider a kind of speech that you often have to deliver: a factual speech where you will be building a logical case. This is a speech in which you are stating some principles at the beginning and proving a point by the end. It's important if you're in situations involving law or political situations; it's important if you're giving a religious speech, a sermon, where you're making a point based on holy writ and carried through to something that applies to modern times; it's important in business, for sales or for promoting the idea of a new activity for your company. In any of these cases, you must build a logical case to be credible.

Susan B. Anthony was an American of the mid-19th century famous for her work trying to secure the vote for women in America. In 1872, she had walked into a barbershop—which was a voter registration place—and demanded the right to register; and when she cowed the people there into submission and did register, she was then accused of a crime and fined $100. She never paid that fine, but starting in the following year she gave the speech that would become her signature speech on the subject of voters' rights.

Library of Congress, Prints & Photographs Division, LC-DIG-ggbain-30124.

Susan B. Anthony built a logical case to illustrate the necessity of women's suffrage.

I'll be reading parts of the speech and then breaking it down as we go so that we can follow the process of her logos, her use of logic, from beginning to end, creating a straight, arrow-like trajectory from the bow to the target.

> Friends and fellow citizens, I stand before you tonight under indictment for the alleged crime of having voted at the last presidential election, without having a lawful right to vote.

That's her introduction; that's as personal as she's going to get. But she needed to explain her relationship to this issue, this logical problem, for you to have belief in her, for her to be credible to you as someone that needs to speak on this point and that you want to listen to. Now she presents the axiom, the unassailable truth on which her argument will be based:

> The preamble of the federal Constitution says: "We the people of the United States."

What's she going to get into now? Definitions of terms; very important to anybody building a logical case:

> It was we, the people; not we, the white male citizens. ... And it is a downright mockery to talk to women of their enjoyment of the blessings of liberty while they are denied the use of the only means of securing them provided by this democratic-republican government—the ballot.

She's already gotten to that hardcore nub of that whole issue: the ballot, the right to vote.

> For any state to make sex a qualification that must ever result in the disfranchisement of one entire half of the people is to pass a bill of attainder, or an ex post facto law, and is therefore a violation of the supreme law of the land.

We continue:

> The only question left to be settled now is: Are women persons? And I hardly believe any of our opponents will have the hardihood to say they are not. Being persons, then, women are citizens; and no state has a right to make any law, or to enforce any old law, that shall abridge their privileges or immunities.

She needed to explain her relationship to this issue, this logical problem, for you to have belief in her.

That is the core of her speech. It is a logical case built step by step, starting with axioms, going on to definitions, going on to examinations and demonstrations of different points, and ending with a conclusion.

In my line of work, I am often called upon to make logical arguments. I have to present my results of my field work to my peers; I have to convince them that the interpretations that I am coming to with my evidence are things that they would agree with. I give a completely different kind of talk at our national meetings when I am with my peers in this science of archaeology than when I'm out on the road giving speeches to groups at museums or civic organizations: I emphasize the logic. When you are making a logical case, as you will be in so many situations in your life, you, too, are going to want to bring people along with you by emphasizing the right part of your argument—the solid, firm footing—and not the softer terrain. ■

Take-Away Points

1. Use clear, concise, but neutral reasoning. Avoid personal issues and emotional appeals.

2. Base your argument on axioms, laws, self-evident truths; present them near the beginning of your speech.

3. Define your terms, and make those definitions into stepping stones as you work toward proving your point.

4. Focus on proving a single point; rigorously avoid side issues and unnecessary digressions.

5. Be strong and forceful, but at the same time, always be courteous and positive and avoid statements that might alienate someone unnecessarily.

6. Check the accuracy of your facts.

7. Think carefully before including humor, anecdotes, vivid language, metaphors, or dramatic surprises in your speech.

8. Enliven your argument with rhetorical questions to create a sense of dramatic dialogue and to clarify opposing issues.

Build a Logical Case—Susan B. Anthony

Lecture 7—Transcript

Welcome back. As we continue to consider how you should be crafting your speech, we're going to move from our subject last time, which was about the architecture and structure of your speech with its tripartite form—beginning, middle, end—and we're going to consider today a kind of speech that is often something you are going to have to deliver: a factual speech where you will be building a logical case. This is a speech in which you are stating some principles at the beginning and proving a point by the end. It's important if you're in situations involving law or political situations; it's important if you're giving a religious speech, a sermon, where you're making a point based on holy writ and carried through to something that applies to modern times; it's important in business, for sales or for promoting the idea of a new activity for your company. In any of these cases, you've got to build a logical case to be credible.

We can go back to Aristotle for some guidance on the kinds of appeals that work in a logical case. He gives us three; very handy as an echo of our subject last time. Aristotle's three appeals are: logos, ethos, and pathos. Logos is reason; logos means "the concept." The ethos is an appeal to personality. He thought of it as an appeal to your own personality—"You should believe me because I'm a good and honorable person"—but it can also be extended to the idea of ad hominem attacks; that is, an attack on the other man, the other person. Ad hominem; you are at your antagonist, and talking about that character and saying, "Don't believe any of that because of the kind of person that is." Obviously this is a weaker argument than the logos, the reason, the logic; and, of course, "logic" comes from that word "logos." Third, there is pathos, the appeal to the emotions. As we're going to see, it makes you a much weaker person in presenting your argument if you base it on the ethos, the personal element, or the pathos, the emotional element, rather than the logos. What we're going to focus on today are good examples of building a speech on logos and some contrary examples where people will use the ethos or the pathos instead, and I believe not be so convincing.

We're going to start with our featured guest professor today, Susan B. Anthony, American suffragette of the mid-19th century who was famous for her work trying to secure the vote for women in America. She gave this speech many times. In 1872, she had walked into a barbershop—which was a voter registration place—and demanded the right to register; and when she cowed the people there into submission and did register, she was then accused of a crime and fined $100. She never paid that fine, but starting in the following year she gave this speech, which became her signature speech on the subject of voters' rights, what she had done, and sets out to prove in a very logical way that she was in the right. I'll be reading parts of the speech and then breaking it down as we go so that we can follow the process of her logos, her use of logic, from beginning to end, creating a straight, arrow-like trajectory from the bow to the target so that we start with some principles, we end with a conclusion that she feels is irrefutable, and if she's done her work you will feel the same way.

> Friends and fellow citizens, I stand before you tonight under indictment for the alleged crime of having voted at the last presidential election, without having a lawful right to vote. It shall be my work this evening to prove to you that in thus voting, I not only committed no crime but, instead, simply exercised my citizen's rights, guaranteed to me and all United States citizens by the National Constitution, beyond the power of any state to deny.

That's her introduction; that's as personal as she's going to get. But she needed to explain her relationship to this issue, this logical problem, for you to have belief in her, for her to be credible to you as someone that needs to speak on this point and that you want to listen to. Now she presents the axiom, the unassailable truth on which her argument will be based:

> The preamble of the federal Constitution says: "We the people of the United States, in order to form a more perfect union, establish justice, insure domestic tranquility, provide for the common defense, promote the general welfare, and secure the blessings of liberty to ourselves and our posterity, do ordain and establish this Constitution for the United States of America."

I don't know if she read that from a book or not, but it would certainly be appropriate for her to take that up in a book and read it to you as a listener; it would be appropriate for you as a speaker when you are giving your axiom or axioms, those bedrock truths on which your argument will be based, to read them. It gives you something to do at the beginning of the speech with your hands; it ensures that you will exactly quote the original words; and the audience will feel more confident seeing that these axioms come from a printed source and not from your own memory.

Now back to Susan B. Anthony. What's she going to get into now? Definitions of terms; very important to Aristotle, very important to anybody building a logical case:

> It was we, the people; not we, the white male citizens; nor yet we, the male citizens; but we, the whole people, who formed the Union. And we formed it, not to give the blessings of liberty, but to secure them; not to the half of ourselves and the half of our posterity, but to the whole people—women as well as men. And it is a downright mockery to talk to women of their enjoyment of the blessings of liberty while they are denied the use of the only means of securing them provided by this democratic-republican government—the ballot.

Alright, here's the problem; it comes from the definition: "We" is in the Preamble to the Constitution; it's not limited in some way—she points that out—it's not just "white males" or even just "males," it's "We the people"; that must include females. In the definition of the term she is beginning to work out the strength of her argument that's going to lead to her conclusion.

Now we move on; she's already gotten to that hardcore nub of that whole issue: the ballot, the right to vote.

> For any state to make sex a qualification that must ever result in the disfranchisement of one entire half of the people is to pass a bill of attainder, or an ex post facto law, and is therefore a violation of the supreme law of the land. By it the blessings of liberty are forever withheld from women and their female posterity. To them this government has no just powers derived from the consent of the governed. To them this government is not a democracy. It is not a republic. It is an odious aristocracy; a hateful oligarchy of sex.

This is the body of her speech; this is the presentation of the whole problem as it's going to be presented to you in the course of the evening, and she is making it very forceful with those short phrases. You heard that; the threes that we saw last time are so helpful: "not a democracy," "not a republic," and here, the third, is the contrary, "an odious aristocracy." That word "oligarchy" means "government by the few"; so she's taking a very technical term, "oligarchy," and yoking it to a very downright term, "sex," "the oligarchy of sex." This is the way to hold your viewers' interest; this is to make your argument seem very immediate.

We continue:

> Webster, Worcester, and Bouvier all define a citizen to be a person in the United States, entitled to vote and hold office.
>
> The only question left to be settled now is: Are women persons? And I hardly believe any of our opponents will have the hardihood to say they are not. Being persons, then, women are citizens; and no state has a right to make any law, or to enforce any old law, that shall abridge their privileges or immunities.

That is the core of her speech. It is a logical case built step by step, starting with axioms, going on to definitions, going on to examinations and demonstrations of different points, and ending with a conclusion. Note that she continues her definitions right to the end: Webster, Worcester—I believe that's how it's pronounced, "Worcester," it might be "Worcester" if he's an American writer—and Bouvier, they are writers of dictionaries. She sweeps you along with this. I want to point out that there's, in fact, an illogicality here: "Webster, Worcester, and Bouvier all define a citizen to be a person in the United States, entitled to vote and hold office." Alright, but she needs to get right on to her great thunderclap of a question—Are women persons?—before we stop to think, "Wait a minute, that definition can be limited to men." She is using the forms of legal argument, even when the logic has to make a big jump there (and Aristotle would have considered this point very illogically arrived at). You saw it again earlier when she used that term "ex post facto," that Latin legal term, to again give a sort of a halo of the legal, of the clear, the concise, the completely logical about the words regardless of what the line of the reasoning might be. Throughout the speech, she's given no examples, she's given no colorful languages, no metaphors, no images, no pictures of oppressed women; it's all been on a cerebral, abstract, intellectual level. That is where logical cases need to be made; as soon as you get off into ethos and pathos, the personal and the emotional, you are beginning to create doubts in your audience's mind about the hard core value of your reasoning.

I want to say that I have edited this speech to give it to you now; she did not originally give it quite this way. There was a digression in the middle and there was a sentence tacked on at the end that I think seriously undermined her own case. Let's go back now and look, having seen a good example of how to make a logical case, how to build it step by step—she still had her three elements there: the introduction, the body, and the conclusion—but let's see some things that were in the original speech that think we should all learn from and decide we're not going to follow that path. First, the digression; this picks up with those words "a hateful oligarchy of sex":

> … an oligarchy of wealth, where the rich govern the poor.

This is the kind of digression that starts trains of thought in people's minds as they try to work it out. There are rich women, there are poor women, there are poor men; where do we tie this in to this whole argument about sex being what she's talking about, that it's about all women? This is not well thought out; this is a distraction, and it's going to disrupt the reader's own concentration, or the listener's own concentration, down this path of, "How does wealth and poverty tie into this?" But now we get into what I really find not just a digression that distracts but something downright offensive; and trust me: You never want to offend any potential listener in the course of a logical case.

> An oligarchy of learning, where the educated govern the ignorant, or even an oligarchy of race, where the Saxon rules the African [where is she going with this, you wonder?], might be endured [what?]; but this oligarchy of sex … carries dissension, discord and rebellion into every home of the nation.

This is a terrible digression. She's weakening her own case; she's saying, "Oh, there are cases where equality doesn't matter so much to me." Is she really saying that the ignorant are not persons? Is she saying that Africans are not as much persons as women? She hasn't thought this through; this should have been cut once it was written as she read through her speech and left on the floor as something not to be put in, both because of the distraction from the main point and of the potential of undermining her own case with an illogicality and of offending some of her listeners.

Finally, let's listen to the original ending of this speech. You'll remember that I gave you her last sentence as this: "Being persons, then, women are citizens; and no state has a right to make any law, or to enforce any old law, that shall abridge their privileges or immunities." That's a strong ending. That's tying the whole thing together; that's going back to the idea of the law of the land that she started with, an echo of her quoting of the Preamble to the Constitution and denying the right of the states to abrogate that. What did she originally go on to say? This is the original ending:

> Hence, every discrimination against women in the constitutions and laws of the several states is today null and void, precisely as is every one against Negroes.

Why did we bring that in? It's an important point, but it's not the point she's trying to make; and to end with that suddenly turns your attention, undercuts everything she said before, and leaves a new case and a new problem in your mind, especially with that very unfortunate echo back to the digression—which I omitted when I read it to you the first time—where she's saying she thinks it's more important for women to have the vote than even Africans. Those are the things that I think are needed to be pruned away in order to make this the really strong argument that it essentially is; although it does have that funny jump in that final definition where she's taking her idea of citizen as a person—" Are women persons?"—from dictionary definitions that don't fully bear out her case. But that brings us to another point I want to make before we leave Susan B. Anthony, and that is you don't want to make cases against yourself. No case is cast iron; every case, even in science and nuclear physics, has contrary opinions and views to present. Let someone else present those unless you can overcome them; unless you have the proofs that show that these contrary views are wrong, leave them out.

Let's talk about the axioms, and let's consider the fact that axioms can show up in all kinds of conversation, in all kinds of presentations, in all kinds of tone. Jane Austen—who we quoted before from *Mansfield Park* and her wonderful observations on the importance of training young people to memorize poetry and speeches and recite them at home so that they can become good speakers—also gives us a good example, although a rather satirical one, of starting with an axiom. The first sentence of her novel *Pride and Prejudice* is an axiom: "It is a truth universally acknowledged, that a single man in possession of a good fortune must be in want of a wife." The whole novel flows from that axiom, and in a very comic way, the way a logical case will flow from the axioms at the beginning of it. Be on the lookout for these when you hear people giving speeches; look for the axioms at the beginning. As you set out to build a logical case, do what Susan B. Anthony did: State what this is about and how it relates to you, but immediately, then, get to your axiom.

On the same subjcct of women's suffrage we can listen to John Stuart Mill in 1867 speaking in Parliament in London. He had married a suffragette—he admired her a great deal—and he, too, is going to give a big speech, as Susan B. Anthony did, about women's rights to vote. Let's hear his axiom right at the beginning:

> To lay a ground for refusing the suffrage to anyone, it is necessary to allege either personal unfitness or public danger.

That is John Stuart Mills's axiom drawn from English law that says that any voter can only have the vote taken away in case of insanity or criminal activity that makes them a convicted felon. He goes on; having stated his axiom, now he's beginning to work out truths from it:

> Now, can either of these be alleged in the present case? Can it be pretended that women who manage an estate or conduct a business—who pay rates and taxes, often to a large amount, and frequently from their own earnings—many of whom are heads of

> families, and some of whom, in the capacity of schoolmistresses, teach much more than a great number of male electors have ever learnt—are not capable of a function of which every male householder is capable?

So he starts with an axiom, and then he tries to find the illogicality between the current situation and the axiom that is part of the law. I think that we can see a problem here in John Stuart Mills's presentation—just as we saw something that I consider a problem with Susan B. Anthony's—and that is that immense parenthesis that is so important for his argument it actually should have been a series of separate sentences. The parenthesis goes—he's talking about the women—"Can it be pretended that women who manage an estate or conduct a business," paying "rates and taxes," and so on; all of those should have been separate sentences, maybe somewhere else in the talk. But it's too much; you've lost the thread of his idea and of his original sentence by the time you get way down to the point where he hooks back up to the "Can it be pretended that" these women are not capable of a function. He's given so many examples that you, the listener, are beginning to lose the thread. You never want the audience to lose the thread of a logical discussion. In entertaining speeches, even in teaching speeches, rambling, discursive, following the subject down all sorts of byways, getting into digressions, they can be a lot of fun. These speeches are not about fun; these speeches are about logos, concept, logical trains of thought (trains as in one car hooked up to the next). You never want to go off into such a long set of examples or a parenthesis that the train of thought is broken, and I certainly think it is broken here.

Also, he makes a mild joke; I don't know if you saw that. But he's talking about why the women should not be considered unfit to vote. He talks about the many women who are heads of families: "and some of whom, in the capacity of schoolmistresses, teach much more than a great number of male electors have ever learnt". That's a joke; that does not belong in this argument. It's also a problem for a second reason: There are going to be some in the Parliament who are thinking, "Is he talking about me? Is he thinking that I am one of those people who were taught more than I learned?" If so, you have some of your audience thinking, "Maybe he's insulting me." You do not want to insult your audience while making a logical case, or any part of your audience. You want to always be courteous, you want to always be positive; treat them as reasonable people who you know are going to do the right thing once they have simply understood the axioms, the definitions of terms, and the logic behind your presentation. Although both Susan B. Anthony and John Stuart Mill, I think, in general teach us a lot of very positive things, I think we can also see some dangers that we want to stay away from as we get into our own public speaking and building our own cases.

To go to someone who was working on this side of the Atlantic in a very different sort of social sphere but back in the same period—in fact, in the year 1876—let's listen to the words of Chief Joseph of the Nez Perce Indians out in the Great Plains. His tribe is being forced onto a reservation and he is resisting with logic. His logic, which comes in the early part of the speech, you won't hear it, is that the Creator—what is sometimes called the Great Spirit in Native American oratory; we're going to hear a lot about that next time as we get into painting a picture in words and listen to the words of Tecumseh, a chief of the Shawnee—Chief Joseph's logic is the Creator gave that land, created the land, for the Indians, and the proof of that is they were the first occupants. Didn't the Creator spread people around the globe? He must have meant the land for this people.

Native American oratory, Indian oratory, is often characterized by flamboyant images, pictorial kind of talking; he really stays away from that here. It's interesting to me that Chief Joseph, who spoke very good English, chooses to use the word "Creator" to identify his supreme being with that of the Christians he's talking to rather than "Great Spirit," which implies that there are two different gods. Here we go:

> Perhaps you think the Creator sent you here to dispose of us as you see fit. If I thought you were sent by the Creator, I might be induced to think you had a right to dispose of me. Do not misunderstand me, but understand fully with reference to my affection for the land. I never said the land was mine to do with as I choose. The one who has a right to dispose of it is the one who has created it. I claim a right to live on my land and accord you the privilege to return to yours.

That's very simple, but it's very powerful; and by avoiding distracting images, poetical language, and any emotion except pride and self-respect, and according that same self-respect to the American official that he's addressing with that final line—I "accord you the privilege to return to yours"; that is, the words of courtesy, although certainly not the underlying emotion—he is building a more powerful case than if he were resorting to appeals about himself or based on emotions about what was owed to his tribe. He is getting back down to axioms: The axiom is the Creator made the world, he assigned people their lands; you do not have the right to change the Creator's disposition of people upon their lands; a very strong case.

Finally, let's hear Chief Joseph getting worked up over the causes of freedom and what he would be within a new United States system. Three years have gone by, this has made a tremendous difference for the status of the Nez Perce—they've lost some battles—but he's still fighting. Here are his logical statements:

> Let me be a free man, free to travel, free to stop, free to work, free to trade where I choose, free to choose my own teachers, free to follow the religion of my fathers, free to talk, think and act for myself—and I will obey every law or submit to the penalty.

He is coming to a legal point and he is stating the conditions now: If he is granted the freedoms, he will accord the obedience to the law; if he is not accorded those freedoms, he will not. Again, no extraordinary images; pure logos, pure reason, as Chief Joseph works us through his ideas on what it will take to make him a loyal citizen of the United States.

In my line of work, I am often called upon to make logical arguments. I have to present my results of my field work to my peers; I have to convince them that the interpretations that I am coming to with my evidence are things that they would agree with. I give a completely different kind of talk at our national meetings when I am with my peers in this science of archaeology then when I'm in the classroom with my students or when I'm out on the road giving speeches to groups at museums or civic organizations: I emphasize the logic. I begin with certain premises that I can demonstrate are true; I make steps one after the other that involve the defining of terms, the establishment of strata; I use a language that is technical—remember Susan B. Anthony using that legal language—I'm using the language of my field in order to get people to buy into what I'm saying, to convince them that the point I'm making is true. I always think in the logical terms; I keep the poetry out of it; I keep the illustrations out of it, how wonderful I felt; I keep myself out if it as much as possible except to say, "These are the conclusions I draw," "This is the evidence that I saw as I excavated that site." If I don't make it logical, I know people will not be with me on my conclusions. When you are making a logical case, as you will be in so many situations in your life, you, too, are going to want to bring people along with you by emphasizing the right part of your argument—the solid, firm footing—and not the softer terrain.

We have a lot of lessons today, drawn from mainly Susan B. Anthony and John Stuart Mill, as we look at the way to build a logical case in a speech. Let's start looking at those lessons: First, use clear, concise, but neutral reasoning (Aristotle's logos). Avoid personal issues, emotional appeals; that is, ethos and pathos. Appeals like that may sway a crowd, but they are most often going to undermine your credibility. Second, base your argument on axioms, laws, self-evident truths; present them near the beginning of your speech. Third, define your terms, and make those definitions into stepping stones as you work towards proving your point. Fourth, focus on proving a single point; rigorously avoid side issues and unnecessary digressions. Unless you can decisively refute objections to your case, do not refer to such contrary matter as you make your speech.

But we have more than this: In addition to those hard, core lessons, there are some others, applying especially to the kind of way in which you present your speech that I think are very important to bear in mind. Be strong and forceful, be an advocate for your view, don't hesitate to make it clear you believe this; but at the same time, always be courteous and positive and avoid statements that might alienate anyone who would be listening unnecessarily. Then, check the accuracy of all your facts; double check the precise meaning of any technical terms that you use in your speech. In addition, think carefully before including humor, anecdotes, vivid language, metaphors, or dramatic surprises in your speech. They're often very good in some kinds of speech; they're not good in arguments. Finally, our eighth lesson for the day, enliven your argument with rhetorical questions—Are women persons?—to create a sense of dramatic dialogue and to clarify opposing issues.

I believe if you can learn from our great guest professors, if you can take to heart what they show you about the step-by-step progression of building a logical speech, your logic will be able to prevail in almost any argument that you choose to make.

Paint Pictures in Words—Tecumseh on Unity

Lecture 8

Over the first three lectures of this part of our course, this middle part on crafting your speech, we've been considering big questions of structure and overall form. What I want to talk about today is something that we agreed wasn't very appropriate to those logical arguments that were the focus of our last lecture: painting pictures in words.

I think the best person to introduce us to the concept of painting pictures in words is Tecumseh. He was a great Indian leader of the Shawnee tribe, a war leader during their wars against the United States in the early 19th century. Tecumseh, more than any other speaker I know—and he was very much part of a longstanding oral tradition—shows us how powerful images, pictorial language, concrete examples, and even imagined dialogues can be.

In 1811, he was trying to rally the Indian tribes, and he's talking to them—the Osages, and later the Choctaws and the Chickasaws—about the importance of Indian unity. Observe the vividness and concreteness in his speech:

> Where today are the Pequot? Where are the Narragansett, the Mohican, the Pocanet, and other power tribes of our people? They have vanished before the avarice and oppression of the white man, as snow before the summer sun. … Sleep no longer, O Choctaws and Chickasaws, in delusive hopes. … Will not the bones of our dead be plowed up, and their graves turned into plowed fields?

With this kind of very pictorial language, Tecumseh is holding the interest of his listeners in two very specific ways: One is when he gives you a very concrete example that is a real-world example of something that he sees is going to happen. He doesn't just tell you, "We shall be defeated by our enemies and lose our land, and will we not then have this problem of our tribal lands and all of our revered tombs of our ancestors being desecrated?" He wants you to feel it: "Will not the bones of our dead be plowed up, and their graves turned into plowed fields?" This is powerful. A simple prediction that there would be trouble ahead or there would be desecration of land doesn't carry this kind of power; and this is what ultimately rallied the tribes behind him to join in a unified effort to save Indian land east of the Mississippi River.

© Photos.com/Thinkstock.

Tecumseh used pictorial language and metaphors to make his message powerful.

But what I really am impressed with in Tecumseh is his genius for picking metaphors. A metaphor is a figural piece of language, a figure of speech, where you use one image to represent another. He talks about how these peoples walk the same path, slake their thirst at the same spring, sit around the same council fire—they are actually sitting around that same council fire at the moment. He calls on a lifetime of experience; the walking the same path, the slaking the thirst at the same spring are metaphors for being all one people. Tecumseh is putting them in terms you can picture, images that you can easily remember and hold in your heart that seem to call on a commonality of experience and really enhance, really reinforce his meaning.

That's a metaphor; but there's also the simile where he's saying one thing is like another. In that beautiful roll call of the dead tribes—where are they? where are the Pocanet; where are the Mohican?—he ends with an extraordinary simile worthy to come out of the *Iliad* or the *Odyssey*, which are a pair of books full of similes: It's the moment where he says, "They have vanished … as snow before the summer sun." To make it a metaphor, he would have said, "They were the snow before the summer sun"; the simile is "as snow" or "like the snow." In either case, we are getting the richness, the power of that image to give new life, and a much longer life, to the thought that's imbedded in Tecumseh's words. To me, he ranks with Lincoln among the greatest American orators of the 19th century. ■

Take-Away Points

1. Focus the attention of your listeners with words that create images in the mind.

2. Use poetic language to make your words easy to recollect and more evocative of memories, of feelings, of shared experience with your audience.

3. In logical arguments or technical explanations, use metaphors to help your listeners "see" a problem or a situation more clearly than they would with an abstract, nonmetaphorical explanation.

4. Don't mix your metaphors, and make sure your metaphors are appropriate for the particular occasion and audience.

5. Make abstract observations and principles vivid to your listeners by adding concrete, easy-to-picture examples.

6. Energize your presentation by imagining dialogue and dramatic confrontations.

7. Apply images and vivid language when you are speaking from the heart.

Paint Pictures in Words—Tecumseh on Unity

Lecture 8—Transcript

Welcome back. Over the first three lectures of this part of our course, this middle part on crafting your speech, we've been considering big questions of structure and overall form. We've looked at storytelling, narratives as something that can give form to your words. We've looked at the tripartite structure, which really should lie behind almost every speech—the introduction, body, and conclusion—and then we've looked at the idea of building a logical case, following a single line of reasoning, or Aristotle's word "logos," from beginning to end of your talk.

What I want to talk about today is something that we agreed wasn't very appropriate to those logical arguments that were the focus of our last lecture: painting pictures in words. I think the best person to introduce us to that concept is a great Indian leader of the Shawnee tribe, born in my part of the United States. His name was Tecumseh, he was a war leader of the Shawnee during their wars against the United States in the early 19th century, and he, more than any other speaker I know—and he was very much part of a longstanding oral tradition—shows us how powerful images, pictorial language, concrete examples, and even imagined dialogues can be.

Let's start in the year 1810. Tecumseh is addressing William Henry Harrison, United States governor for the old Northwest Territory, and he is making points about Indian rights to their land, about Indian unity, and about the inequity of some Indians being bribed or intoxicated by the Americans so that they will sign away rights to all Indian land.

> Houses are built for you to hold councils in. The Indians hold theirs in the open air. I am a Shawnee. My forefathers were warriors. Their son is a warrior. From them I take my only existence. … I have made myself what I am. And I would that I could make the red people as great as the conceptions of my own mind, when I think of the Great Spirit that rules over us all. I would not then come to Governor Harrison to ask him to tear up the treaty. But I would say to him, "Brother, you have the liberty to return to your own country."

> You wish to prevent the Indians from doing as we wish them, to unite and let them consider their lands as a common property of the whole. You want by your distinctions of the Indian tribes to make them war with each other. You never see an Indian endeavor to make white people do this.
>
> No tribe has the right to sell land, even to each other, much less to strangers. Sell a country!? Why not sell the air, the great sea, as well as the earth? Did not the Great Spirit make them all for the use of his children?
>
> How can we have confidence in the white people? When Jesus Christ came on earth, you killed him and nailed him on a cross. You thought he was dead, but you were mistaken. You have Shakers among you, and you laugh and make light of their worship. Everything I have told you is the truth. The Great Spirit has inspired me.

This is a very antagonistic speech; and yet he has raised issues about human relationship with the divine that put the whole thing on a very different footing than it would be on if he were just appealing to the law of the land and Indian rights as guaranteed by the American government. He wants to raise the ante; he does that with these religious images: invoking Jesus on the cross; Shakers, those early American religious sect members who separated themselves from the main population and were known, as the Quakers were, for their religious trances.

Now we're in 1811, the following year. He's trying to rally the Indian tribes, and he's talking to them—the Osages, and later the Choctaws and the Chickasaws—about the importance of Indian unity. We heard some of his vividness, some of his concreteness in that first speech; now we're really going to get it when he's talking to his own people.

> Brothers, we all belong to one family; we are all children of the Great Spirit; we walk in the same path; slake our thirst at the same spring; and now affairs of the greatest concern lead us to smoke the pipe around the same council fire … The Great Spirit is angry

> with our enemies; he speaks in thunder, and the earth swallows up villages, and drinks up the Mississippi. …

I should say at this point he is referring to the great earthquake, called the New Madrid earthquake, of the years 1811–1812 that he actually, if one believes the speeches, predicted.

> Where today are the Pequot? Where are the Narragansett, the Mohican, the Pocanet, and other power tribes of our people? They have vanished before the avarice and oppression of the white man, as snow before the summer sun … Sleep no longer, O Choctaws and Chickasaws, in delusive hopes … Will not the bones of our dead be plowed up, and their graves turned into plowed fields?

With this kind of very pictorial language, Tecumseh is holding the interest of his listeners in two very specific ways: One is when he gives you a very concrete example that is a real-world example of something that he sees is going to happen. He doesn't just tell you, "We shall be defeated by our enemies and lose our land, and will we not then have this problem of our tribal lands and all of our revered tombs of our ancestors being desecrated?" he wants you to feel it: "Will not the bones of our dead be plowed up, and their graves turned into plowed fields?" This is powerful. A simple prediction that there would be trouble ahead or there would be desecration of land doesn't carry this kind of power; and this is what ultimately rallied the tribes behind him to join in a unified effort to hold onto Indian land east of the Mississippi River.

But what I really am impressed with in Tecumseh is his genius for picking metaphors. A metaphor is a figural piece of language, a figure of speech, where you use one image to represent another. Where he talks about how these peoples walk the same path, slake their thirst at the same spring, now sit around the same council fire, they are actually physically sitting around that same council fire at the moment, but he calls on a lifetime of experience; the walking the same path, the slaking the thirst at the same spring are metaphors for being all one people, but they are putting it in terms you can picture, images that you can easily remember and hold in your heart that seem to call on a commonality of experience and really enhance, really reinforce his meaning.

That's a metaphor; but there's also the simile where he's saying one thing is like another. In that beautiful roll call of the dead tribes—Where are they? Where are the Pocanet, where are the Mohican?—he ends with an extraordinary simile worthy to come out of the *Iliad* or the *Odyssey*, which are a pair of books full of similes: It's the moment where he says, "They have vanished … as snow before the summer sun." To make it a metaphor, he would have said, "They were the snow before the summer sun"; the simile is "as snow" or "like the snow." In either case, we are getting the richness, the power of that image to give new life, and a much longer life, to the thought that's imbedded in Tecumseh's words.

To complete his story: Having become the war leader of the Shawnee, he was in some senses betrayed by his own brother, a prophet, who carried on wars without him and lost them. He eventually fought on the British side in the War of 1812 and died battle, and no one knows where his body lies. Nonetheless, to me he ranks with Lincoln among the greatest American orators of the 19th century.

I think we saw in Tecumseh perfect use of figural language, of poetical, pictorial language. Let's listen to a little bit of an address he might actually have seen a copy of, Thomas Jefferson's inaugural address of 1801 as he's being sworn in as President, to see both some metaphors that get out of control and also then a perfect example of a metaphor that helps an audience focus on the words. Remember, an inaugural address is somewhere between the logical case that we talked about last time where the speech is going to be covering a series of points in an orderly fashion governed by logos, and an inspirational speech where you are trying to get people behind your vision of what's lying ahead in the coming term. Here we are, Thomas Jefferson, 1801:

> During the throes and convulsions of the ancient world, during the agonizing spasms of infuriated man, seeking through blood and slaughter his long-lost liberty, it was not wonderful that the agitation of the billows should reach even this distant and peaceful shore.

Mr. Jefferson, this is too many metaphors for one sentence. We have three at work here, and they are all the more jarring for being metaphors and not similes. First we have "throes and convulsions," "agonizing spasms";

these are metaphors drawn from the world of sickness, of people in fevers and horrible medical conditions. That's where we begin, but suddenly we find them "seeking through blood and slaughter" their "long-lost liberty." This is a contrary image: If you're on the sickbed, you shouldn't be in the next clause, out on the battlefield with a weapon cutting your way through a bloody field. It just doesn't make sense, and we're starting to lose even the grip we originally had on his thought. Finally, by the time we get to the "agitation of the billows" that "reach … this distant and peaceful shore," now we have a nautical image of the waves upon the sea all in one sentence. There used to be a little comic feature in the *New Yorker* magazine—perhaps there still is—called "Block That Metaphor" where examples just like this are picked out of current newspaper and magazine publications where someone's words are quoted, and typically it's three or more of these jostling, jarring, incompatible metaphors all yoked together. One per sentence, as Tecumseh knows, is the right way to go.

Yet at the same time, just a little later in that same inaugural address, we find Jefferson in the quietest, simple way possible elucidating how the view of a leader is different from that of the view of any other person in the country, because the leader has the high ground and sees it all. Here's what he says:

When right, I shall often be thought wrong by those whose positions will not command a view of the whole ground.

This is as simple as a metaphor can be. It is simply talking about those moments when you're high up and suddenly you see the whole countryside spread out at your feet and you understand the relationships between things and the relative positions, as opposed to a person down in the field who can only see a much more restricted horizon and makes judgments based on that limited view. The metaphor is perfect; the idea of the leader in that higher place actually makes a very precise correlation between Thomas Jefferson's highest office in the land and the idea of a person on a physically high place having the wide view and everybody below taking issue because their limited view causes them to draw different conclusions. Thomas Jefferson—I think an example for what we shouldn't do in his mixed metaphor—an example of a perfect metaphorical use of pictorial language to make his speech memorable, and not only that but make it clear at the moment. As soon as one hears that, one feels a little disarmed; one feels, "Gosh, I've been doing that; I've been criticizing leaders. They must see more than I do." The message comes through in the metaphor.

In the Western tradition, a lot of metaphors go back to Homer and to the *Iliad* and the *Odyssey*. Homer belonged to an oral tradition, like Tecumseh; as a college lecturer, I belong in that same oral tradition, and someone who stands up and delivers hundreds or as I think I may have told you probably by now about 2,000 times speeches, lectures, demonstrations, and presentations to people who need to understand knowledge. I want to keep them focused, I want to see them interested, and I want to be sure that they are picturing exactly what I'm picturing, especially if I use technical terms. I turn to the same technique as Homer—the one that we saw Tecumseh using—of employing metaphor or simile so that they get a picture of what I'm talking about. Homer has infinite variety in his use of metaphors and similes. My favorite comes at the end of Book Eight of the *Iliad* when the Trojans have at last burst out of Troy. Achilles, the Greek hero, is sulking in his tent; the Greeks are getting the worst of it; and for the first time in 10 years, Hector is able to lead the Trojans out so that they can encamp for the night in tents and bivouac on their own great plain. Each tent lights a fire, and there are the fires burning on the plain.

It's poetical already, but Homer takes it a step further and tells you, "So shine the stars around the moon on a clear night." That's the watch fires of the tents of the Trojans on the plain around the great central moon of the great city of Troy itself. But he goes further and describes the whole night: the solitude, the quiet, the sound of the shepherd's pipe and the rejoicing of the shepherd's heart as he alone sees this majestic scene of the stars and the moon, and then heaven itself seems to burst open to its uttermost reaches. He doesn't need to do all that; his metaphor is feeding into creating the mood, just as you saw Tecumseh using those specific metaphors. What does "snow before the summer sun" do for you? It suggested something they all know; the passing of a thing that seemed permanent during the winter, but has only too short a lease on life, that snow. Homer is working at the same level as Tecumseh; he's trying to use images from the natural world that everybody can understand and picture in order to reinforce his message.

I'd like to read you a little passage from Homer that is one of my favorites. We're at Book 23 at the end of the *Iliad*, and old King Nestor is trying to tell his son, Pisistratus, how you can win a chariot race if you don't have the fastest horse. What he is using here, Nestor—what Homer is putting into his character's mouth—are a series of images where Nestor is using comparisons. The point is very simple: Nestor is telling his son, "If you want to win the race with slower horses, you're going to have to use craft, art, cunning." We don't have a single word in English for that cluster of things, but the Greek word *metis* means something like "cunning," "intelligence," "art," "craft." I'm just going to use *metis* in this translation that I've made from the *Iliad*. Here's King Nestor:

> To win the prize, keep metis well in mind. By metis, not brute force, men fell great oaks. By metis steersmen on the wine-dark sea steady their swift ships through the tearing gale. By metis charioteer beats charioteer.

There was only one real message—you're a charioteer, you can use this cunning to win—but somehow by evoking the woodsman out in the great forest cutting down the oaks and shaping them and by picturing the pilot, the steersman, at the rudder of the ship trying to guide that ship through the storm, Homer has enlightened the issue, has made through the parallels one feel all the sense of danger and tremendous accomplishment that can come from this use of *metis*, something the Greeks prize, something we don't. But it's the images, it's the concreteness of it, rather than just giving a general rule that makes it memorable and that makes it something that helped Pisistratus to, in fact, come in second in that big chariot race.

As long as we're with the Greeks, I'd like to point out that the Greeks had a great fondness for this kind of use of an example. One of the most familiar elements of Greek culture in our world is *Aesop's Fables*. Aesop was a real person of the sixth century B.C., he lived on the island of Samos, and he collected and in some instances wrote little tiny animal stories like "The Fox and the Grapes" that stick with us as part of our mainstream culture. They were originally used not so much by nursery maids with their little children to entertain them—although that's where I found them, in my preschool books—they were used by orators making speeches in public to make serious points and yet, at the same time, hold the attention of the audience. You've probably heard about the one about "The Boy Who Cried Wolf." A statesman would stand up and say, "Please don't listen to my learned colleague who was just addressing you; he's been claiming that the Persians are going to invade for the last 10 years and they still haven't. He's like the boy who cried wolf who wanted to see what the townspeople would do if he stirred them up; so he would stand out there by the sheep and shout from the hill 'Wolf, wolf!' and they would all come running out. He did it again and again until finally the people didn't believe him, and then when the wolf really came there was no one to come; he was not believed."

Or there would be—to stick with the shepherd—"The Wolf in Sheep's Clothing." Here's an ambassador come; and you are saying he looks very fair and very friendly. He's a wolf in sheep's clothing; his master, the king of that foreign country, is actually out to destroy us. "The Tortoise and the Hare": "Yes, I'm a slow and plodding person, I don't have the brilliance of my colleague; but believe me, I'm to be trusted. I'm like the tortoise that continues to put one step after the other while the hare gets distracted or gets overconfident and is, in fact, overtaken by me at the end of the race." Finally, one of my favorites, not so well-known, about how one person—if they are strong, forceful, and believe in themselves—can really count for much more than a multitude is Aesop's fable about "The Vixen and the Lioness." A vixen (a female fox) laughed at a lioness because the vixen had many cubs and the lioness had one cub. "Yes, only one," said the lioness, "but a lion."

With all of these little images, these little stories, the Greeks would enliven their political discourse; make the crowd interested. There was even a story about how one orator rebuked a crowd because all they wanted to hear were these Aesop's fables; and we know from Plato that when his old master Socrates was in prison waiting for his death sentence to be carried out with the drinking of the hemlock, he spent his days turning Aesop's fables into poetry. They were little nuggets of wisdom, little observations, and pictorial scenes as from a cartoon that you could easily grasp, easily remember, and made a consistent point.

Another great source of beautiful images in poetry that comes out of an oral tradition can be found in the Hebrew Bible in the Psalms, which were some of them written by David himself, a shepherd, and others written for the court of his son, King Solomon. Let's hear Psalm 127 for an example of how you make abstract ideas concrete through images:

> Except the Lord build the house, they labor in vain that build it. Except the Lord keep the city, the watchman waketh but in vain. It is vain for you to rise up early, and sit up late, to eat the bread of sorrows, for so he giveth his beloved sleep. Lo, children are an heritage of the Lord, and the fruit of the womb is his reward. As arrows are in the hand of a giant; so are children of one's youth. Happy is the man that hath his quiver full of them: he shall not be afraid to contend with his enemy in the gate.

I think an exceedingly beautiful thing there is as the flow of the images goes by and you sort of expect them to each be taken up in turn and then dropped, it's a wonderful moment when the children are described as those arrows in the hand of a giant and they show up in the next clause as the householder, the family man, with a quiver full of those arrows, a quiver full of children, surrounded by his children when he meets in the gate (the court) to defend his rights among the people. None of that would stick with you if it was a simple statement of the facts about the necessity of relying on the Lord and on your children to support you in this life; that either seems like a platitude not worth stating, or as something that, among all the other platitudes and rules, you're just not going to focus on. Images make you focus; the things that you picture through the image are things that you will retain and continue to think about and continue, in this case, to be inspired by.

Although I don't encourage the idea of using a lot of images and poetical language and metaphor in the kind of logical speech we were talking about last time, let's listen to one of America's great speakers, Daniel Webster, as he is making a presentation to the jury, to the court, in a murder trial, the trail of John K. Knapp for murder:

> He has done the murder. No eye has seen him, no ear has heard him. The secret is his own, and it is safe! Ah! gentlemen, that was a dreadful mistake. Such a secret can be safe nowhere. The whole

creation of God has neither nook nor corner where the guilty can bestow it and say it is safe!

How powerful that is as Daniel Webster imagines the secret as a physical thing that can be hidden in nooks and corners, and yet truly can never be hidden. We see it, we feel it; we feel the terror of the accused person as that secret is talked about in that way.

Let's close with an example of a speech from 19th-century America that uses vivid language and shows us both how to do it, and then a little later how not to do it. Our speaker is William Jennings Bryan, it's the presidential nomination campaign of 1896, and this is his famous "Cross of Gold" speech. In the middle part of the speech, he uses vivid language in a perfect way:

> Burn down your cities and leave our farms, and your cities will spring up again as if by magic; but destroy our farms, and the grass will grow in the streets of every city in the country.

Such a powerful way of expressing the idea that it is rural America that is the true basis of American strength and prosperity. But at the end of the speech, we sort of go off the deep end. This is what made the speech famous, gave it its name the "Cross of Gold" speech; he's talking about the gold standard, and he gets into biblical language that seems so inappropriate, hyperbolic, and over the top that it's hard for me to believe that it was ever taken as seriously as it seems to have been. Here we go:

> If they dare to come out into the open field and defend the gold standard as a good thing, we will fight them to the uttermost … saying to them, "You shall not press down upon the brow of labor this crown of thorns; you shall not crucify mankind upon a cross of gold."

It's memorable; it's poetical; it has that biblical basis that's typical of so much of the imagery used by American orators; but it is so completely inappropriate—in my view at least—to compare the results of going one way or another on the arguments about bimetallism to the crucifixion of Jesus or to the crucifixion of mankind upon a cross of gold that it's my personal opinion this is why he lost the presidential election. Maybe not; but William Jennings Bryan is best known for that image of the cross of gold.

With all this in mind—how to do it, how not to do it—let's think of some lessons that we can draw from Tecumseh especially, but from all of our speakers about how you may want to as you craft your speech think about ways to express abstract ideas in more vivid form through the language you choose. First, focus the attention of your listeners with words that create images in the mind; in other words, paint a picture with words. Next, in emotional or personal speeches especially—less often in the sort of reasoned argument that we talked about last time—use poetic language, use pictorial metaphors to make your words easy to recollect and make them more evocative of memories, of feelings, of shared experience with your audience. Third, in logical arguments or technical explanations, use metaphors to help your listeners "see" a problem or a situation more clearly than they would with the sort of abstract, non-metaphorical way.

I think we have a few other rules here, too; a few other ideas that we can draw from this discussion of the kind of language that you use to express your ideas. First, a big don't: Don't mix your metaphors; and make sure your metaphors are appropriate for the particular occasion and audience. Second, make abstract observations and principles vivid to your listeners by adding concrete, easy-to-picture examples. That's not necessarily in the world of metaphors or similes, but that's just thinking what this would really look like played out in reality and then citing those examples—those little things, whether they are in fable form or drawn from the newspaper—give examples of how this principle is affecting the real world. Those can either be poetical or they can be kind of homely and ordinary. Next, go beyond rhetorical questions: Energize your presentation by imagining dialogue and dramatic confrontations, as you remember Tecumseh does as he imagines how he will dismiss Governor William Henry Harrison with a bit of dialogue from his own lands. Finally, apply images and vivid language when you are speaking from the heart. Simple abstractions don't convey much meaning on an emotional level; it's the pictures you paint, it's the images you use, that if you are making an appeal to people to something other than their reason—to their emotions, to their deepest-held convictions—it's those images that are likeliest to be remembered long after the sound of your voice has faded away.

Focus on Your Audience—Gandhi on Trial

Lecture 9

There are times when you are talking to people who you know are resistant to what you have to say. One often talks about speeches being meant to persuade. It's not my belief that they often change people's minds in the act of being spoken; they usually just move people from dead center to a position that they are ready to go to.

We are getting ready to get out in front of that audience and speak in public. What I have devised for our last four sessions together is a sequence of speakers who can focus for us on certain essential elements of giving the speech. The first one is the great Indian leader Mahatma Gandhi, with the speech that he gave when he was on trial for his life. This speech is one that illustrates focus on the audience, and it shows us a very difficult case—although not an uncommon one—where there may be more than one constituency that the speaker must bear in mind.

We're in Ahmadabad, India; the year is 1924. Gandhi has been publishing material for Indian youth about his idea of Satyagraha—nonviolent, passive resistance—and has been accused by the occupying British government of sedition, a capital crime. Gandhi was trained as a lawyer. He's used to courtrooms—so you'll see that in part he is focusing on the primary target of his speech, the judge. But Gandhi is aware there is another, and for him more important, audience: the Indian people; the millions who had been following his printed words and who would now follow the speech through the

Gandhi masterfully addressed two different audiences with a single speech.

newspapers. He is thinking about making statements of belief that not only make clear his legal position but make clear his mystical faith in the right of India to be free and in the future of India as a free country.

Gandhi is aware there is another, and for him more important, audience: the Indian people.

In the following excerpts, you can see that this is a speech with no introduction. We are moving into the heart of things with his very first words:

> Nonviolence is the first article of my faith. It is the last article of my faith. But I had to make a choice. I had either to submit to a system which I considered has done irreparable harm to my country, or incur the risk of the mad fury of my people bursting forth when they understood the truth from my lips.
>
> I have no personal ill-will against any single administrator, much less can I have any disaffection towards the King's person. But I hold it to be a virtue to be disaffected towards a government which in its totality has done more harm to India than any previous system.
>
> I am here, therefore, to invite and submit cheerfully to the highest penalty that can be inflicted upon me for what in law is a deliberate crime, and what appear to me to be the highest duty of a citizen.

That's a great speech. It suggests his own pride and self-respect; it suggests the pride in his country that he feels at heart; it encapsulates in its last two clauses the two different targets of his speech. Notice one is directed at the judge: I am here, cheerfully, to accept "the highest penalty that can be inflicted upon me for what in law [you, Mister Judge, will know] is a deliberate crime, and what appear to me [and obviously to his people] to be the highest duty of a citizen." The two audiences, the two tones as it were, are both there.

The tone is very reasoned: He is giving a fair assessment; he is not asking for mercy. He recognizes the role of the judge and what the judge must expect;

and that reasonable tone is, in fact, part of his defense. He, I believe, would have been happy to die—he knows that would have made him a martyr and that would have brought about the much more rapid liberation of India through horrendous wars—but he didn't particularly want to touch off those wars, and so he is, in a way, being conciliatory. He's making it easier for the judge to commute this sentence from death to some sort of penal servitude, and that is indeed what happened. It's a masterpiece of a speech, but it is, I think, one that better than most shows us a speech presented at two different audiences and very clearly satisfying both. ■

Take-Away Points

1. Ask yourself in advance, "Who is my audience?" and adapt your speech to address them particularly and directly.

2. Your tone, your language, and your examples should all be chosen with a specific audience in mind.

3. Always be courteous, respectful, sympathetic, and mindful of your audience's comfort.

Focus on Your Audience—Gandhi on Trial

Lecture 9—Transcript

Welcome back. Over the past eight lectures we have been preparing ourselves and preparing our ideas for a speech in public, and now it's show time. We are getting ready to get out in front of that audience—out of our studies, out of our homes, into the real world—and speak in public. What I have devised for our last four sessions together is a sequence of speakers who can focus for us on certain essential elements of giving the speech. The first one that we are going to bring in as a guest professor is the great Indian leader Mahatma Gandhi, and the speech that he gave when he was on trial for his life. This speech is one that illustrates focus on the audience, and it shows us a very difficult case—although not an uncommon one—where there may be more than one constituency that the speaker must bear in mind as they give their talk.

Let's begin: We're in Ahmadabad, India, the year is 1924. Gandhi, who has been publishing magazine or newspaper for Indian youth about his idea of Satyagraha—that nonviolent, passive resistance that is nonetheless resistance—has finally been accused by the occupying British government of sedition, and that is a capital crime. Gandhi was trained as a lawyer. He's used to courtrooms—in South Africa, where he lived as a younger man, he worked in courtrooms himself—so you'll see that in part he is focusing on the primary target of his speech, the judge; and in the full version of the speech you would have heard him address "Mister Judge" in person several times. But Gandhi is aware there is another, and for him more important, audience: the Indian people; the millions—and I do mean millions—who had been following his printed words and who would now follow the speech through the newspapers, through all of the organs by which it would be disseminated to the people in India who longed for liberty from England. He is thinking about making statements of belief that not only make clear his legal position but make clear his mystical faith in the right of India to be free and in the future of India as a free country.

We begin at his very beginning; and in this case I would say this is a speech with no introduction. We are moving into the heart of things with his very first words:

> Non-violence is the first article of my faith. It is the last article of my faith. But I had to make a choice. I had either to submit to a system which I considered has done irreparable harm to my country, or incur the risk of the mad fury of my people bursting forth when they understood the truth from my lips. I do not ask for mercy. I do not plead any extenuating act. But by the time I have finished with my statement you will, perhaps, have a glimpse of what is raging within my breast to run this maddest risk which a sane man can run.
>
> My experience of political cases in India leads me to the conclusion that in nine out of every ten the condemned men were totally innocent. Their crime consisted in love of their country. This is not an exaggerated picture. Section 124-A under which I am happily charged is perhaps the prince among the political sections of the Indian Penal Code designed to suppress the liberty of the citizen. Affection cannot be manufactured or regulated by law. If one has no affection for a person or thing one should be free to give the fullest expression to his disaffection, so long as he does not contemplate, promote or incite to violence. I have no personal ill-will against any single administrator, much less can I have any disaffection towards the King's person. But I hold it to be a virtue to be disaffected towards a government which in its totality has done more harm to India than any previous system.
>
> In fact, I believe I have rendered a service to India and England by showing in non-cooperation the way out of the unnatural state in which both are living. Non-violence implies voluntary submission to the penalty for non-cooperation with evil. I am here, therefore, to invite and submit cheerfully to the highest penalty that can be inflicted upon me for what in law is a deliberate crime, and what appear to me to be the highest duty of a citizen.

That's a great speech. It suggests his own pride and self-respect; it suggests the pride in his country that he feels at heart; it encapsulates in those last two clauses the two different targets of his speech. Notice one is directed at the judge: I am here happily, cheerfully to accept "the highest penalty that can be inflicted upon me for what in law [you, Mister Judge, will know] is a deliberate crime, and what appear to me [and obviously to his people] to be the highest duty of a citizen." The two audiences, the two tones as it were, are both there.

He does have that extraordinary bit of humor in his speech. I think this is very much not for the judge but for the people to show his carelessness; this is like the condemned man whistling a tune on the scaffold just before the little ramp opens below him and he falls to his death with a noose around his neck. That business about "Section 124-A under which I am happily charged"—that "happily" is a warning we have something satirical coming—"is perhaps the prince among the political sections of the Indian Penal Code"; these are not the words of someone who is afraid of his fate; this is someone who is willing to, in fact, give a rude gesture at the occupiers of India to the delight of all those who are going to be reading this speech.

Nonetheless, the tone is very reasoned: He is giving a fair assessment; he is not asking for mercy; he recognizes the role of the judge and what the judge must expect; and that reasonable tone is, in fact, part of his defense. He, I believe, would have been happy to die—he knows that would have made him a martyr and that would have brought about the much more rapid liberation of India through horrendous wars—but he didn't particularly want to touch off those wars and so he is, in a way, being conciliatory: He's making it easier for the judge to commute this sentence from death to some sort of penal servitude, and that is indeed what happened. It's a masterpiece of a speech, but it's, I think, one that better than most shows us a speech presented at two different audiences and very clearly satisfying both.

There are times when you are talking to people who you know are resistant to what you have to say. One often talks about speeches being meant to persuade. It's not my belief that they often change people's minds in the act of being spoken; they usually just move people from dead center to a position that they are ready to go to, or intensify a mood that is already there. But I'd like to read you an example of a speech that was given in the hope of convincing a very unsympathetic body to vote in a way contrary to the mood in which they had entered the chamber. This was a speech given in the United States Senate in 1847. The speaker is Thomas Corwin, a senator from Ohio, and he is trying to convince the President of the United States not to follow those who want to tear territory away from Mexico, which has been recently defeated, and make it part of the United States. There are many issues here behind the scenes—enlarging the number of slave-owning states, states where slavery was legal, is part of it—but Corwin really doesn't want this to happen, and he's trying to find a way to stop what has become a trend in America, that Manifest Destiny that is carrying America relentlessly towards the Pacific Ocean. How's he going to do it? The speech didn't work, but I think he found the right tone. Let's hear his words:

> What is the territory, Mr. President, which you propose to wrest from Mexico? It is consecrated to the heart of the Mexican by many a well-fought battle with his old Castilian master. His Bunker Hills and Saratogas and Yorktowns are there! The Mexican can say, "There I bled for liberty!"

That's a stroke of genius; there were still people alive in the United States 1847 for whom the American War of Revolution was a living memory, and certainly the majority of the people who formed the government at that time had at least fathers, if not grandfathers, who'd fought at Bunker Hill or Saratoga or Yorktown. He is getting on undeniable ground here when he compares their feelings toward the struggle toward liberty of the American Revolution toward what those Mexicans feel about the land that is now being taken away from them. As I say, it didn't work; but it's the right way to go about trying to change your audience's mind through your speech: Once you know that your audience is antagonistic, look at what they feel favorably toward, and then try to align the subject of your speech with that favorable impulse; glorify your own subject through attaching it to something that they glorify themselves.

We also have Theodore Roosevelt to help us in this same position of you're talking to a potentially unsympathetic audience. Roosevelt, in 1902, went to New York City to help open a grand new building to house the Chamber of Commerce. There were many dignitaries present for this huge celebration, it was one of the landmarks of New York, and the Chamber of Commerce was among the most important, wealthy, influential bodies of men in the country. Roosevelt at this time, like Corwin half a century earlier, had an issue on his mind: the issue of unions, the rights of laborers, as opposed to these plutocrats who sat in New York at places like the Chamber of Commerce and seemed to pull all the strings in the country. His speech is a little bit of a Trojan horse. I'm not going to read you all the sections that are long congratulations to the Chamber of Commerce for everything that they've done, but I assure you that most of the speech is about praising them, praising their role in American history. Nonetheless, he is tucking in his conviction that until there's a balance between the wealthy and the laboring classes America will not truly live up to its potential. Let's listen to how he does it; Theodore Roosevelt, at the New York Chamber of Commerce:

> Important though it is that we should have peace abroad, it is even more important that we should have peace at home. You, men of the Chamber of Commerce, to whose efforts we owe so much of our industrial well-being, can, and I believe surely will, be influential in helping toward that industrial peace which can obtain in society only when … employer and employed alike show not merely insistence each upon his own rights, but also regard for the rights of others, and a full acknowledgment of the interests of the third party—the public. … No patent remedy can be devised for the solution of these grave problems in the industrial world, but we may rests assured that they can be solved at all only if we bring to the solution certain old time virtues.

If he had come to the podium, President Roosevelt, and said, "I'm going to make an appeal here for more rights for unions," I think people would have been throwing things at him. He's wrapped it up in such a way as to make his message as acceptable as possible. First of all, he's praised them; he's praised them for their role in American history and in bringing America to this pinnacle of power and wealth. He goes on at the very end of that passage that I quoted to tie them to old-time virtues; that they represent that old-time, traditional quality, those good American virtues of thrift, of hard work, of fighting for independence. They are banner-carriers; they should be the ones to set an example. He's, in fact, trying to flatter them into changing their attitudes towards the laboring masses, towards the unions, towards giving the workers a fair share of say in their own destiny and in America as a whole. There were mixed results from this speech—you're well aware that struggles between management and labor are still part of our American scene—but he didn't shy away from making the attempt, he just had the good sense to phrase his oratory, his rhetoric, in such a way that rather than a blunt demand or a statement of his own position that would alienate his audience, he made every effort possible to make it easy for his audience to say, "We might agree with that."

That was a powerful man addressing some of the wealthiest in the country; let's turn the coin over and look at a man, a priest, way back in 1381 in England talking to a lot of peasants at Blackheath, outside London, about overturning their political order and see how he matches his tone, his language to that particular audience. The man's name is John Bell, he's the man who touched off the Peasants' Revolt, and he's well aware that those who are rallying to the cause are, in many cases, peasants themselves; not just idealists and reformers like himself, but peasants who have been used to working in the fields, yoking the animals to the plow, bearing the burden of English economies on their shoulders and not getting any rewards from it. He wants to reach them on their own level, and we will see how he brings in imagery and kinds of speech that he thinks will make a direct appeal to them.

> When Adam delved and Eve span, who was then the gentleman? From the beginning, all men by nature were created alike, and our bondage or servitude came in by the unjust oppression of naughty men. For if God would have had any bondmen from the beginning, he would have appointed who should be bond, and who free. … The time is come for you to cast off the yoke of bondage, and recover liberty.

He began with a little rhyme. Most of his listeners are illiterate, they don't know books, so he is wanting to reach out to them with the kind of literary reference they might actually be familiar with: a sort of nursery rhyme, "When Adam delved and Eve span, who was then the gentleman?" What does this mean? He's referring back to those Bible stories they would have heard in church about Adam and Eve thrown out of the Garden of Eden and becoming the first workers. There were no gentlemen then, there was no one to do the work; Adam is farming, digging the fields—we're told this in the book of Genesis—and Eve is spinning cloth to make them clothing in order to hide their nakedness. They are workers; he is identifying his listeners, his audience, with the primal couple in all of human history, Adam and Eve. This is a way of giving them pride in what they're doing; but he's making a serious point in addition: There were no gentlemen then, nobody worked for anybody else; God did not so arrange the world that Adam and Eve were a lord and a lady. They were workers; that is the natural, original status of human beings. He asks the question: Who was then the gentleman? There was no gentleman; and he makes the point that neither bondage nor gentlemen came in until these high men oppressively forced it on weaker, lower men.

I also like his use of the word "yoke," "yoke of bondage." That's kind of a dead metaphor in most speeches about liberty, you find it in lots of the speeches that go along with the Revolutionary War; in other words, "the yoke of oppression," "the yoke of slavery" has been used so often, what we say by dead metaphor is you've forgotten that it really means an object from the agricultural world, that wooden or leather contraption that goes over the neck of the ox or the other draft animal so that the plow can be pulled. He brings it back to life, that dead metaphor, by using it to a group of peasants who have just come off the farm, who have just left their plows behind them and are now getting that reinforcement from him: Cast off this yoke, cast off this symbol of your oppression, join me in the attack on the established order; a beautiful speech; a beautiful use of metaphor.

Let's stick with English history for a moment and go back to someone we've had already as a guest professor: Queen Elizabeth I of England. We last encountered her at Tilbury Field trying to rouse up the courage of her troops to face the Spanish Armada. Thirteen years later she received a deputation from the House of Commons in Parliament and she wanted to talk to them about her relationship to them and her love for the common people of England. To picture the scene as it was at the beginning of this short excerpt, you need to realize that they would have not been allowed to stand in her presence unless she gave them leave. As soon as they came into the presence of their monarch, they had to get down on one knee, lower their heads, and not look at her until she gave them leave to do so, and typically that would not be until the end of the speech. This is a speech of thanks, this is a speech of warmhearted love for her subjects, and she gives the impression halfway through—and I'm going to only ready you a part from the middle—that she's realizing that she has so much to say about her love for them that she's going to go off the script; and so we have this interesting little piece written into the speech that the queen gives:

> Of myself I must say this, I never was any greedy scraping grasper, nor a strict fast-holding prince, nor yet a waster, my heart was never set upon any worldly goods, but only for my subjects' good. What you do bestow on me I will not hoard up, but receive it to bestow on you again. Mr. Speaker, I would wish you and the rest to stand up, for I fear I shall yet trouble you with longer speech. To be a king, and wear a crown, is a thing more glorious to them that see it than it's pleasant to them that bear it.

That's a short excerpt from a long speech, but that moment where she first of all breaks off and says, "Stand up; I'm going to talk so long I know you won't be able to hold that proper pose, I want you to be able to hear all the things that I have to say of thanks and praise for you"; and then the little thing aimed very much at them—she certainly wouldn't say this to another monarch—that "You who look at me think it's more glorious to wear this crown than I do, who wear it," that is a monarch talking to common people, that's trying to put herself in touch with their point of view and perhaps correct it from her own perspective, but always thinking about them. There's never been, I don't think, a monarch in the world quite like Elizabeth, and she was rewarded with a love from her people that certainly matched the kind of love that she showed for them.

We certainly have in America presidents who've shown an instinctive kind of empathy with the people of America, and one of the most striking of those was John Kennedy. He, through a series of speeches—I think everyone remembers even if one was not alive at the time that he used that famous line about, "Ask not what your country can do for you, ask what you can do for your country"—reached out to people; he wanted people to be getting in touch with and getting involved with their own government, their own country's health and state of affairs; he wanted an inclusive government, and so his words were a testimony to that. He also wanted to get Americans behind the idea of the space exploration program, and I want to play a little clip, and let you hear a little clip, of Kennedy talking about this quest to get a man on the moon that he used as a speech in a number of different places, but you're going to be hearing him at Rice University, standing in the football stadium. Let's listen to him for a little bit, and then I will share with you something that the president of Rice University told me about what Kennedy said that day.

> We choose to go to the moon. We choose to go to the moon. We choose to go to the moon in this decade and do the other things, not because they are easy, but because they are hard, because that goal will serve to organize and measure the best of our energies and skills, because that challenge is one that we are willing to accept, one we are unwilling to postpone, and one which we intend to win, and the others, too.

That's a beautiful line, that you should undertake a thing not because it is easy but because it is hard. I hope you noticed at the beginning of that clip, from the center of what is quite a long speech by President Kennedy, that use of threes—"We choose to go to the moon, we choose to go to the moon, we choose to go to the moon"—he almost pretends that he said it three times just to be heard over the crowd's applause; nevertheless, the triad, the triple repeat, is something we talked about as a way of really reinforcing any kind of a message. But I hope you also noticed at the very end of that clip where he tossed in almost in an undertone "undertaking this and the other things, too" how that weakened the statement, the same problem that we saw with the end of Susan B. Anthony's original speech. When you've made your point, stop talking; and, of course, someone who did sometimes extemporize and go off script the way President Kennedy would do, the way I think we saw Queen Elizabeth doing, is sometimes going to make decisions that perhaps are not optimal for the occasion.

I was told by Rice University President David Leebron that Kennedy actually in addressing a group there while he was on campus said something that didn't end up in the final official version; he said to them all, "Why does Rice play U.T.?"—meaning: "Why does Rice University's football team play the football team of the University of Texas at Austin?"—and then he followed that by his same essential message about the glory of the space program:

"Not because it is easy, but because it is hard." Everybody at Rice got the message immediately; they all understood that idea, because they feel, too, that it's always unlikely that they shall beat the University of Texas—they're a small liberal arts college—nonetheless, they all feel the glory of having attempted an immense, seemingly impossible task and occasionally achieving it. They were also impressed—as David Leebron shared with me and has become part of Rice tradition apparently—that Kennedy knew exactly where he was, knew exactly who he was talking to, and threw in to almost casual conversation a reference to something, calling it U.T., that they would all get, would be the way they would say it themselves, and felt honored then correspondingly from the President of the United States immersing himself in their own point of view and in their own interests.

Let's go to a very different kind of speech at the Harvard Commencement ceremonies of 1978. The speaker was the great Soviet writer and activist Alexander Solzhenitsyn; a very different tone here as befits the man, and perhaps in a way befits the place. Let's just hear the opening of his Commencement address:

> I am sincerely happy to be here with you on the occasion of the 327th commencement of this old and illustrious university. My congratulations and best wishes to all of today's graduates.

So much for his introduction; now, the body:

> Harvard's motto is "Veritas". Many of you have already found out and others will find out in the course of their lives that truth eludes us as soon as our concentration begins to flag, all the while leaving the illusion that we are still pursuing it. Also, truth is seldom sweet; it is almost invariably bitter. A measure of bitter truth is included in my speech today, but I offer it as a friend, not as an adversary.

This is not the tone that they expected, and yet I think they must have felt as he went on with a speech that was in part critical of things in the Western world that they were being honored by him, they were being respected by him. Certainly he feels absolutely on an equal level with Harvard University and all of its grand traditions. Notice that little tiny touch at the beginning,

"I am sincerely happy to be here with you"; I'm sure 99% of the graduation speakers at Harvard, Yale, Princeton, and the other great universities say, "I am honored." He didn't feel that they had any honor to bestow on him; it was he who could bring a mutual sense of equality and of honor on both sides to the occasion. Then there is that bit of the timing of his theme for his speech, truth, to their motto; that's the same kind of thing that Kennedy had done, that he's remembered for at Rice, of having picked up on an obsession of people at Rice from the president right down to the freshman class, the annual game with U.T. By showing he'd studied enough to know about them, he paid them a great compliment and he also, then, had a springboard for his speech. He had that word "veritas," "truth," and he made that the keynote of his own address, and thus created a very memorable, a very powerful speech as well as a recognition of Harvard, important enough that he would study it before he came; that this great man of letters would really get to know the place where he was speaking.

I urge you, whenever you are talking to a group, be sure that you talk to them having studied them, having gotten to know them. If there are relevant links that you can draw between your experience and theirs or between your subject and the things that concern them, do so; personalize, particularize your speech for the audience at hand. I have a very vivid memory of being invited to be a commencement speaker at a high school in Louisville, the Collegiate School, where my dear sister Amy was a student at one time. It was a school that ran from 1st grade to 12th grade, and many of the graduating seniors had heard me give lectures there at the school. I was honored to be invited to be their speaker, but I was aware that the 1st graders, and the 2nd and 3rd, were all going to be there because they all came to the ceremony; I didn't want to leave anybody out.

First of all, I went around to where the 1st graders were gathering before the ceremony, and I told them a little story about my own family: I have a great-nephews named Jack, and Jack's mother—my niece Carol—told me that on one occasion Jack, when he was three or four, having been told a hundred times by his mother, "You're not listening, you're not listening," made it plain to her that she'd been on the wrong wavelength the entire time when the two of them were lying in bed one morning hearing the rain on the roof and Jack suddenly turned to her and said, "Am I listening?" He hadn't understood. They all thought that was funny, more a joke on the mother than on the kid; and so I said, "OK, I'm going to be giving this long speech. I'm going to try to make it interesting for you, but every now and then I'm going to shout, '1st graders, are you listening?' and what are you going to say?" They all shouted back at me right then, "We're listening." So periodically through my address, which went on about 20 minutes and I'm sure would have bored them stiff if they had not been keyed up to participate, I would ask them, "1st grade, are you listening?" "We're listening." I enjoyed it, they enjoyed it; I had no idea about the rest of the assembly, but it was a way of reaching out to a group in the audience—and a pretty sizeable one when you threw in the other young grades—who otherwise might have felt completely left behind. At the same time I used some of my own experiences in the field to draw a picture of young people in old societies who were kept by their elders from going out in the morning until they heard some truths, and said that I was one of those elders standing at the door and making sure that before the young people ran out of the lodge they would hear some of the truths that I wanted to share with them. In this way, I'd hoped to touch everybody in that audience.

Let's consider: What are some of the lessons we can learn starting with our great guest lecturer today, Gandhi, but thinking of all of these different people and different kinds of speeches we've heard that show a very keen appreciation on the part of the speaker for the audience? First of all, you must ask yourself in advance, "Who is my audience?" and you must adapt your speech to address them particularly and to address them directly. You must remember that you may have two or more constituencies among your listeners; be sure to address them all. Not only your message, but your tone, your language, and your examples should all be chosen with a specific audience in mind. And, you need to look for areas of common ground with your listeners; that's the way to bring them over onto your side, and that's the way to make them feel that that you have respect and interest in what they are feeling. Finally, unless you are determined to alienate your listeners, always be courteous, respectful, sympathetic, and—like Queen Elizabeth—mindful of their comfort.

Share a Vision—Martin Luther King's Dream

Lecture 10

We're going to do a sort of anatomical analysis to understand why this speech by this minister from a church in Atlanta, Georgia, was nominated by the journalists of the *Guardian* newspaper in London in the year 2000 as the most important and influential speech of the 20th century.

In this lecture, we study a very different kind of speech with a different emphasis: the famous "I Have a Dream" speech by Martin Luther King Jr. I think it's important to remember that a speech needs a principle tone, and the tone that pervades Martin Luther King's speech is the tone of ethos, the personal feeling. This is a speech that I think you should take as your model when you're thinking about speeches that are meant to be inspirational.

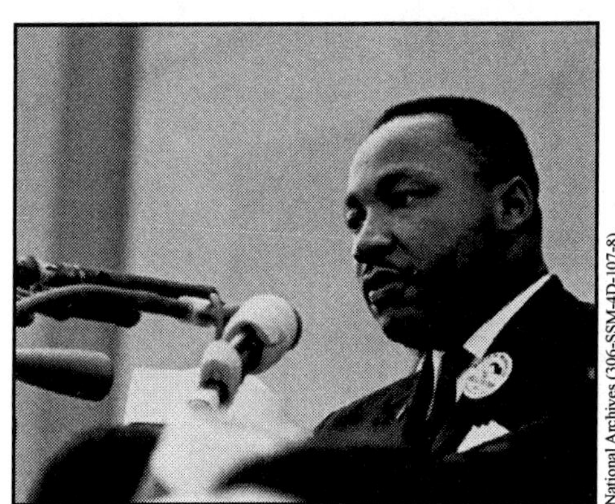

National Archives (306-SSM-4D-107-8).

Martin Luther King Jr. shared a vision that ultimately became a reality.

The year is 1963; we are standing with hundreds of thousands of people outside the Lincoln Memorial on the National Mall at Washington DC. Martin Luther King Jr. has his back to the Lincoln Memorial, which contains not only the great statue of Lincoln seated but also quotations from the Gettysburg Address and the Second Inaugural Address. Lincoln is the great emancipator; Martin Luther King wants to evoke his spirit immediately in his speech, and he does it without even naming Lincoln. How?

Here is the first sentence of Martin Luther King's speech: "Five score years ago, a great American, in whose symbolic shadow we stand today, signed the

Emancipation Proclamation." What a thought-provoking way to make the audience connect this present occasion with what happened in the Civil War 100 years before; that war that was fought over the issue of slavery, and that had not yet brought to a full resolution equal rights for all Americans.

He begins to work his way through other ideas, broadening the original application of the fact that an essential injustice and oppression has been done, touching on some of those actual oppressive acts, but in general staying away from that. If you're trying to inspire people, follow Martin Luther King's example: Do not use negatives to try to create a positive. He rigorously excludes from almost the entire speech any specific references to the outrages, the indignities, the criminal acts that have been done in the effort to deny African Americans their rights; instead, he is relentlessly positive. Relentless positivism makes people feel, no matter what your exact words, that they want to be with you as you work your way through to your conclusion.

It's at the end of the transition that we suddenly find him talking about dreams—the American Dream, his own dream—and now comes that second part of the speech, the one that is stuck in everybody's minds. This is where the dream begins to echo through the speech, resound like the ringing of a bell again and again.

> I have a dream that one day this nation will rise up and live out the true meaning of its creed [and now he stops his own words and quotes the Declaration of Independence]: "We hold these truths to be self-evident, that all men are created equal."

He goes through a number of other dreams, but at the heart of this litany comes the heart of the ethos, the heart of the personal vision: He is actually going to describe for you his dream for his own family; you can't get more intimate than that:

> I have a dream that my four little children will one day live in a nation where they will not be judged by the color of their skin but by the content of their character.

That is powerful, not only because it's so personal but because of a simple device: alliteration.

As he goes on, he begins to work away from the dream, and with another transition he moves toward the third part of his speech, the pathos, where we are going to be in the realm of emotion. He sees a mystical thing: a gigantic mountain, whittled down to a single small stone. The mountain was despair, but what has been carved down out of it is hope. That's a beautiful image. He also has another image—although this one is one that you would hear—discords, conflicting sounds gradually being transformed into brotherly harmony as the whole world learns to sing together.

He is actually going to describe for you his dream for his own family; you can't get more intimate than that.

That's his transition to the pathos, the emotional part of the speech, and this for him is as important clearly as the ethos where he's ringing the bell of "I have a dream"; now we are getting into the world of a different phrase, "let freedom ring." At the end, he has a short conclusion to wrap it all up; and in his conclusion, having brought together these opposites, reconciled all the conflicts, he sees all the people gathering together and singing, in the words of a traditional spiritual hymn:

> Free at last! Free at last! Thank God Almighty, we are free at last!

He gives that line from the spiritual, "Pride of Place," as the resounding conclusion of his speech; again, not his own words, just as he started not with his own words, but somehow resting on a higher authority. It's a wonderful speech. That man's vision ultimately did become a reality; it partly became a reality because of that speech. This is one of those speeches that we can say made a difference to history, to the way an entire country thought about the issue. When you're trying to inspire people, look at this speech. I do not know any better example of how to put together an extended speech that deals with stirring up positive feelings in a group of people and making them go forth renewed and thanking you for sharing your inspiration with them. ■

Take-Away Points

1. Integrate all three kinds of appeals—logic, personal concerns, and emotions—if you want to make your most satisfying and most compelling case.

2. If you want to create the feeling of visions, repeat words and phrases.

3. Weave familiar quotations and references to well-known texts into your speech.

4. Divide a long speech into three clear-cut sections; give each section its own particular tone and its own particular take on your theme.

5. Maintain eye contact with your audience, and maintain your energy while reading quotes. Use pauses and changes in vocal tone to set the quotes apart from your text.

Share a Vision—Martin Luther King's Dream

Lecture 10—Transcript

Welcome back. In this last section of our course on the art of public speaking, you will remember that we are focusing on the actual delivery of the speech to a live audience, and on the relationship that you are going to want to establish between yourself and the audience as you deliver, read, or extemporize those words that you have decided to use to clothe your ideas and put them across most effectively. We've also been talking systematically about Aristotle's three kinds of appeals: the logos, which is the appeal to reason; the ethos, the appeal to the personality, especially of the speaker; and finally the pathos, the appeal to feelings. Last time, in our first of these four lectures, we focused on Gandhi, a former lawyer now on trial for his life in the speech we heard, and that speech really showed how the keynote that he sought to strike was the keynote of logos, reason, orderly thought. In this way, he could both appeal to the judges—his primary audience—and also to the millions of Indians who would be listening because remember, nonviolence is the beginning of his faith, nonviolence is the end; he's wanting people to use this reason rather than force or rage in dealing with this long-term injustice in British India.

Today, we are looking at a very different kind of speech with a different emphasis: the famous "I Have a Dream" speech by Martin Luther King, Jr. I think it's important to remember that a speech needs a principle tone just as it needs a single, focused subject and just as it needs a sense—although it may be broken into three parts—of a single trajectory from the first word to the last. The tone that pervades Martin Luther King's speech is the tone of ethos, the personal feeling, and that's expressed in that phrase that has come to be known as the title of the speech, the "I Have a Dream" speech. As we'll see, that's not the biggest part of the speech and it's not the first part, but it is the element that dominates the rest, that gives the rest of the speech a special color. This is a speech that I think you should take as your model when you're thinking about speeches that are meant to be inspirational, motivational; speeches that will work on people's visions of the future because you have shared your own vision with them. It's not so much about closely reasoned argument (although it needs some of that to be a balanced speech) and it's not so much about the pathos, the working on emotions in a general way (although it needs that also), it's about a personal vision. We have a word in our language, "inspiration." It comes from the Latin *inspiratio*. The "in-" is "inside," the "-spiratio" as in "respire" and so on, that means "breath"; your spirit, your breath is inside you. You want to share it now, you want to put it into other people; you're going to do that with words.

This is a long speech. It is in the traditional three parts; each of the three parts emphasizes one of Aristotle's three kinds of appeal. Let's think for a moment about the architecture of the speech. Martin Luther King, Jr. was a minister by training. His father had been a minister. He was used to sermons that needed to last for a very long time, and needed to somehow have this structure as they worked their way through from a beginning, often with a biblical text—that would be the sort of axiom that starts the whole logical process off—working up to personal statements on the part of the clergyman, and finally that universal application that is the pathos, the feelings, at the end where the audience may be moved to stand up to join the speaker in what can be called a "call and response" tradition in those churches where the minister will call out, shout out, give a line and the people respond; that kind of joining together in a mutual emotion was often a climax.

What we're going to focus on in this speech as we work our way through it is that section that has remained in the public mind as the real focus of the speech: "I Have a Dream"; the ethos, the personal vision being shared as the inspiration of the speech. I think it's interesting to note that most people you will talk to about this speech have no idea that it began with a long, logical section—we'll get to that in a moment—with a very carefully worked out metaphor that compares guaranteed freedoms to, of all things, checks written out or drawn on a certain bank; not what you'd expect in this speech if you didn't already know it, and certainly not something that's lodged in the popular memory, but a very necessary part of Martin Luther King's progression. The middle of the speech is the "I Have a Dream," the ethos; that's what everybody remembers, it's so compelling. The whole idea of a dream being part of the American style of looking at life is mentioned by Martin Luther King himself; that he felt that his dream was a subset of the American dream or grew out of the American dream. Many people through history haven't had this obsession with dreams; we as Americans do, and this speech is the ultimate expression of that. Finally, there's a third section, the actual conclusion of the speech, better remembered than the first but often still forgotten by people who think about the speech only in terms of that ringing repetition, "I have a dream, I have a dream"; and that is a section of the speech working on general emotions by quoting a famous song and then taking the last line of that song and using it as a refrain, repeated in a litany of clauses in order to build up the same kind of force, but now not just about the speaker and the speaker's dream but about the whole country united in a final great burst of emotion.

So let's take the speech and begin to work our way through it; we're going to do a sort of anatomical analysis to understand why this speech by this minister from a church in Atlanta, Georgia was nominated by the journalists of the *Guardian* newspaper in London in the year 2000 as the most important and influential speech of the 20th century, an extraordinary achievement on Martin Luther King, Jr.'s part; let's see how he did it.

First of all, we want to set the stage: The year is 1963; we are standing with hundreds of thousands of people outside the Lincoln Memorial on the Mall at Washington, DC, our nation's capital. Martin Luther King, Jr., himself is a well-known figure; he has not yet received the international glory that came to him when, the following year, he was awarded the Nobel Peace Prize. We've had a number of Nobel Prize winners among our great speakers; maybe that shows that they go together. At any rate, his back is to the Lincoln Memorial; and as you may know, on the inside of the Lincoln Memorial is not only the great statue of Lincoln seated but engraved, carved, on the walls quotations from "The Gettysburg Address" and from "The Second Inaugural Address," so that he is able to evoke Lincoln. We're going to be with Lincoln on our very last speech, number 12 in the series of lectures that we're devoting to public speaking; but everybody knew those words, everyone knew who Lincoln was, and everybody knew that Lincoln had begun his "Gettysburg Address" with the words "Four score and seven years ago," a very biblical, a very evocative way of saying "87 years ago." Exactly 100 years had gone by since Lincoln pronounced those words at Gettysburg. Lincoln is the great emancipator; Martin Luther King, Jr. wants to evoke his spirit immediately in his speech, and he does it without even naming Lincoln. How does he do it?

Listen to a direct quote of the first sentence of Martin Luther King's so-called "I Have a Dream" speech: "Five score years ago, a great American, in whose symbolic shadow we stand today, signed the Emancipation Proclamation." Even without the more clear reference to Lincoln, just using "Five score years ago" to say "100" is a very thoughtful way, and a very thought-provoking way, to make the audience connect this present occasion with what happened in the Civil War 100 years before; that war that was fought over the issue of slavery, and that, in Martin Luther King Jr.'s opinion and that of many others, had not yet brought to a full resolution equal rights for all Americans.

This first section is going to be the logos part of Martin Luther King's speech. After evoking Lincoln, he gets into—what I have to say when I first read it was a very surprising to me—kind of reasoned argument about what was the problem in America today. He picked a source of imagery through a metaphor, an extended metaphor. What's that mean? You may know Shakespeare's sonnet "When to the sessions of sweet silent thought / I summon up remembrance of things past"; it goes on for another 12 lines, but throughout those other 12 lines there's continual courtroom imagery. Shakespeare loved to do this; he liked to, like Homer, picture one thing always in terms of something else, and so he's picked his image (the courtroom) and to his own delight and amusement figured out all the ways in which thinking about a love affair can be like being in court. Martin Luther King is going to do the same kind of balancing act in this opening section of his speech—which is, in fact, the first two-thirds of the whole speech—this reasoned argument; not a reasoned call for action, not a reasoned call for the future, he's not going to give us that in this speech. This speech is going to be a vision of the future, the Promised Land that lies ahead, without a road map on how to get there; but he wants to set up the initial situation and he does it through his extended metaphor: this metaphor of the bad check.

Let's get into his logos, his reasoned section of the speech. This source of imagery that is going to be so common begins as sort of an axiom: He's going to quote for us what lies behind his bad check metaphor, the founding documents of our country; and he will quote lines from—or at least allude to—the Constitution and the Declaration of Independence; and later on he's going to actually quote a direct line from the Declaration of the Independence. All the way through this speech he's going to be quoting not just single lines but entire texts of songs and other familiar quotations as he builds up his whole grand edifice on the words, on the images, on the evocative statements and verses that other people have created. We have our axiom, we have our ground to stand on, guarantees: the Constitution, the Declaration of Independence. That's the first step; the second step is to say these guarantees have been violated, this is an assertion. It's to say that while the guarantees are being filled for some, they are not for others; injustice, oppression are preventing the guarantees from being offered to the general public, that portion of the general public that is African American, which is excluded by race and has been for the 100 years since the Emancipation Proclamation of Abraham Lincoln from enjoying those guarantees. Now we get the metaphor: It's a bad check; everybody else is able to cash their check, but this group—these hundreds of thousands—have come to Washington, DC, check in hand, to try to cash it and they're finding that the bank is claiming to have no money and their check will be stamped "insufficient funds."

I'm not sure that this was the best kind of metaphor to use. I want to suggest to you that the reason the public has forgotten this part of the speech is because it is intellectual; it involves a lot of logical reasoning, it involves remembering the details of the check metaphor as you go along and get to the bank, and get to the words that are stamped on the check and what they mean; and then the conviction of the African Americans that there are plenty of funds to cash this check. This is not true, the bank is lying to them; they should receive those funds. I think perhaps in the mental effort to try to follow the picture—the extended metaphor's becoming almost an allegory here; that is, a metaphor turned into a story—you have to imagine that people are beginning to stop listening to whatever he's saying at that moment and start to focus on working out what's just been said in image form. Whether I'm right about that or not, this did not become the remembered, the well-beloved part of the speech; nonetheless, it is the opening statement and it starts it off on that mood of logos, reason, logic. Let's follow with him step by step, from axioms and statements of self-evident truths that no one will deny and see where that lands us.

Having gone through his extended check metaphor, the bad check, he wants to make a transition now to what's going to be the big part of the speech, the

"I Have a Dream" speech; and so he is going to begin to work his way through other ideas, through other concepts, broadening the original application of the fact that an essential injustice and oppression has been done, touching on what some of those problems are, some of those actual oppressive acts, but in general staying away from that. If you're trying to inspire people, follow Martin Luther King, Jr.'s example: Do not use negatives to try to create a positive. He rigorously excludes from almost the entire speech any specific references to the outrages, the indignities, the criminal acts that have been done in the effort to deny African Americans their rights; instead, he is relentlessly positive. We saw that already in Gandhi, we're going to see it again with Mark Antony and Lincoln, our other two speakers in this section, that relentless positivism makes people feel, no matter what the exact words are you're saying, they want to be with you as you work your way through to your conclusion.

It's at the end of the transition that we suddenly find him talking about dreams—the American Dream, his own dream—and now comes that second part of the speech, the ethos; it's the shorter part, but the one that is stuck in everybody's minds. I just want to draw a parallel back to what I'd mentioned regarding Winston Churchill when he gave the world, it would seem, the conventional triad of terms "blood, sweat, and tears"; as we remember, he didn't really say that, he said, "blood, toil, tears, and sweat." The popular consciousness rejected that, picked out what it wanted, made three of it, and that became "blood, sweat, and tears." Similarly, with this speech by Martin Luther King, that long first section is often simply left out when the speech is excerpted in shorter form and certainly has not made its way into the popular consciousness. Was it a mistake to put it in? No; everybody's expecting a long speech. Some of these people have walked to get there; there are hundreds of thousands of them from all over the south; it's been a long journey. They are aware that they are there at a moment of great importance, great significance both to American history and specifically to African American history; the length of the speech needs to match that. Remember, Lincoln could only get away with a three minute address at Gettysburg because someone else—who we will briefly meet in our last lecture, Edward Everett—had already given a two hour oration. Martin Luther King has to shoulder the burden of presenting a speech of such gravitas, such weight, such critical mass that people are aware the speech lived up to the occasion.

And he's starting low; he's starting with the emotional level very controlled, he's starting with a metaphor that you find is thought-provoking rather than inspiring or stirring up your strong emotions so that he has somewhere to go. In a way, the trajectory of a fairly long time on that level plane to begin with and then the stair steps accelerating gives a feeling of drama, gives a feeling of dynamism to the other two portions of the speech. As I said, this second portion is the ethos, is the section where he opens his heart (ethos being, as Aristotle would say, all about you; all about the speaker or personalities at any rate). This is where the dream begins to echo through the speech, resound like the ringing of a bell again and again. We're, in fact, going to hear that phrase "I have a dream" eight times. There are going to be six elements to the dream, or six individual dreams; at two of them, he repeats at the end that phrase, "I have a dream."

> I have a dream that one day this nation will rise up and live out the true meaning of its creed [and now he stops his own words and quotes the Declaration of Independence]: "We hold these truths to be self-evident, that all men are created equal."

We have our element of logos here, our element of reason and logic; but now we have gone to a more exalted place: We're in a dream; we're in one of those prophetic visions, like those of Isaiah or Amos in the Bible. He is creating a nimbus, a sort of aura, of light and magic around these words by this continued refrain, "I have a dream."

He goes through a number of other dreams; as with the Old Testament prophets, a lot of the things he sees in the dreams are geographical. If you read through the prophecies in the Hebrew Bible, the Old Testament, you'll find that again and again they give a concrete reality and grounding to the dream by naming the place where it happened. We're going to hear three states mentioned specifically as part of the sequence of dreams or visions: Georgia, Mississippi, Alabama; he's foretelling transformations in each one of those states, each of them separate dreams. But at the heart of this litany, this sort of repetitious sequence of prayer-like or religious-inspired statements, there comes the heart of the ethos, the heart of the personal vision: He is actually going to describe for you his dream for his own family;

you can't get more intimate than that. Here we are, another direct quotation from his work:

> I have a dream that my four little children will one day live in a nation where they will not be judged by the color of their skin but by the content of their character.

That is powerful, not only because it's so personal—often public figures like to keep their children out of the limelight, and he's brought them right into the thick of things—but by a very simple device, one of dozens that are talked about for effective rhetoric: this alliteration, especially at the beginning of words, "the content of their character," the "color of their skin." Those repeated "cuh" sounds, the "c" or the "k" in "skin," bind that phrase together; it makes it seem like something you would encounter in a vision, something out of those biblical verses where the King James translators often sought for that kind of alliteration to give verbal impact, aural impact (the way you hear it in your ear) to the sequence of words.

As he goes on, he begins to work away from the dream, and with another transition he moves toward the third part of his speech, the pathos, where we are going to be in the realm of emotion. This brief sort of transitional phase gets biblical again with two terms we met back in our lecture where we talked about Paul the Apostle and his sermon or letter on the quality of *agape*, charity or love; you will remember at the very end of that Paul takes one by surprise by bringing in a threesome, but two of the elements we haven't heard about before: faith and hope. Martin Luther King knows the entire Bible by heart; he is now picking faith and hope out as things that he will evoke—the unspoken love is hovering in the background—and so he works his way through hope to faith and begins to talk of all the things he has faith in, about the transformative power of faith. He actually begins to have his own visions again, like a prophet. He sees a mystical thing: He sees a gigantic mountain, whittled down or carved down to a single small stone. The mountain was despair, but what has been carved down out of it, through much work, is hope, a small stone of hope. That's a beautiful image. He also has another image—although this one is one that you would hear—discords, horrible noises, conflicting sounds gradually being transformed into brotherly harmony as the whole world learns to sing together.

That's his transition to the pathos, the emotional part of the speech, and this for him is as important clearly as the ethos where he's ringing the bell of "I have a dream"; now we are getting into the world of a different phrase, "let freedom ring." Those are not his words; he is going to give you the entire text of a familiar hymn (I sang it when I was at Green Valley Grade School, watching the flag right after the Pledge of Allegiance):

> My country, 'tis of thee,
> sweet land of liberty, of thee I sing;
> land where my fathers died,
> land of the pilgrims' pride,
> from every mountainside let freedom ring!

He immediately seizes upon that quotation, "let freedom ring," for another rhythmic litany, like the "I have a dream" one that's preceded and been the middle part of the speech; "let freedom ring," and we're back to our geographical terms.

One of the things that he saw in his dream, his sequence of dreams, was a vision that he takes straight out of the prophet Isaiah. It's from the Advent part of the liturgical year in the Christian calendar—that's when it's most usually read, this vision—it's the vision of the world's changing when it's put right by the coming of the righteous one. Isaiah puts it in terms of these great geographical, geological changes. As Isaiah says (I want to read you the King James version of the passage):

> Every valley shall be exalted, and every mountain and hill shall be made low: and the crooked shall be made straight, and the rough places plain:
>
> And the glory of the LORD shall be revealed.

The visions bounce off each other as Martin Luther King, Jr. starts proclaiming again and again, "Let freedom ring, let freedom ring." What is it ringing off of? Isaiah's hills and mountains; and so he does a litany of hills and mountains, some of them by name, in different states: We get New Hampshire, New York, Pennsylvania, Colorado, California, Georgia,

Tennessee, and Mississippi all named, some of them with the appropriate mountains—like Lookout Mountain for Tennessee—echoing Isaiah, binding the visions together, making you feel this great world all singing, all resounding, letting freedom ring with Martin Luther King Jr.'s vision.

At the end, he has a short conclusion to wrap it all up; and his conclusion, having brought together these opposites, reconciled all the conflicts, he sees all the people gathering together and singing, in the words of a traditional spiritual hymn that he must have heard, again, often in his father's church and in his own, and now quoting from the hymn:

> Free at last! Free at last!
>
> Thank God Almighty, we are free at last!

He gives that line from the spiritual, "Pride of Place," as the resounding conclusion of his speech; again, not his own words, just as he really started not with his own words but with ideas from the Constitution and the Declaration of Independence, but somehow resting on a higher authority. It's a wonderful speech; it's a wonderful example of how to weave together quotations, different sources, words from the Bible, from songs. One thing I want to remind you about when you are using quotes is it's a very good thing to have the book. You want to be sure you can find the correct quote quickly without having to fumble for it or search the page, but you also want to keep up your energy level through the quote and you want to keep the eye contact with the audience. Try to memorize—and if you watch the films you'll see he really kept up the eye contact—the opening of the quote and the end so that at the beginning and as you come out of it you are able to still be with your audience, putting it over to them, communicating with them every second.

That man has shared a vision. That vision ultimately did become a reality; it partly became a reality because of that speech. This is one of those speeches that we can say made a difference to history, to the way an entire country thought about the issue, partly because of that essential positive element in the speech and partly by skimming over exactly how are we going to do this? It wasn't a ways and means kind of speech; it's sharing a dream, sharing a vision. When you're trying to inspire people—whether it's a group of people at work, whether it's your family, whether it's people at a eulogy in church or during a sermon, whether it's a group of athletes who are being coached by you—whatever the inspiration is being applied to, look at this speech. I do not know any better example of how to put together an extended speech that deals with stirring up positive feelings in a group of people and making them go forth from that place renewed and thanking you for sharing your inspiration with them.

I'd like to consider the ways in which Martin Luther King had an impact beyond his own time and in different areas of the United States. Let's consider an American president who, in fact, I believe drew on that tradition that Martin Luther King, Jr. had made familiar to the whole country: those simple phrases, the repetitions, the sort of rhetorical style of the sermon and the appeal. I'm talking about President Ronald Reagan. The year was 1987. President Ronald Reagan had gone to Berlin to challenge the existence of that wall. His speech writers were debating on whether he should mention the idea that the wall should be torn down, and he decided at the very last minute to do so. Let's listen to him using those effects from Martin Luther King in his speech.

> There is one sign the Soviets can make that would be unmistakable, that would advance dramatically the cause of freedom and peace. General Secretary Gorbachev, if you seek peace, if you seek prosperity for the Soviet Union and Eastern Europe, if you seek liberalization: Come here to this gate! Mr. Gorbachev, open this gate! Mr. Gorbachev, tear down this wall!

President Reagan enjoyed many triumphs in the course of his presidency, but none greater than that; and the entire city of Berlin seemed to join in the effort.

Let's conclude by looking at our lessons, mainly drawn from Martin Luther King's "I Have a Dream" speech, and considering what we can take away from this lecture on inspiration. First of all, it helps to integrate all three kinds of appeals, logos, ethos, and pathos—appeals to logic, appeals to personal concerns, and appeals to emotions—if you want to make your most satisfying and most compelling case. But specifically in inspirational speeches, second, the personal and emotional elements are far more important than the logical; visionary images carry more weight than reasoned argument. If you want to create the feeling of visions, repeat words and phrases; this will create a powerful feeling of unity, inevitability, whether you do it at a pregame pep talk, a political rally, or even a religious revival. But we have some other elements, too, that we want to remember. Do what Martin Luther King, Jr., did: Weave familiar quotations and references to well-known texts into your speech; this establishes common ground with your audience. Also, divide a long speech into those three clear-cut sections that we've been striving for all through the course; give each section its particular tone and its own particular take on your theme. Finally, maintain eye contact with your audience and maintain your energy while reading those quotes, especially at the beginning and the end of the quote. Use pauses and changes in vocal tone to set the quotes apart from your text.

It may not be your own words that you are using, but believe me you will infuse your words with additional and especially spiritual power if you will bring in the best of the words of others.

Change Minds and Hearts—Mark Antony

Lecture 11

It is the province of knowledge to speak and it is the privilege of wisdom to listen.

—Oliver Wendell Holmes

Our main focus in this lecture is on pathos—appeals to emotion—in the great speech that Shakespeare wrote for the historical character Mark Antony in the play *Julius Caesar.* This very famous speech begins, "Friends, Romans, countrymen," and may be the most quoted speech in the history of theater. Mark Antony is ostensibly buying into the idea that the assassination of Caesar was necessary, that Caesar was ambitious to become a monarch or a tyrant, and that what the conspirators did was just. In his heart, he is wanting to work on the emotions of the crowd, who've been convinced by the previous speeches of Brutus and the others that what was done was just; he wants to bring them over to a sense of outrage, he wants to turn the crowd against Brutus and the other conspirators.

I consider this to be the hardest thing in public speaking. It's the rarest thing in the world to actually figure out how to change a crowd's opinion. These are Shakespeare's words, remember—we don't know exactly what the original Mark Antony said—but Shakespeare has given us a model on how to work on people's emotions to change their fundamental attitude to a situation. We start with the strongest beginning of any speech I know. It immediately grabs the attention; it identifies the speaker with the audience by calling them "friends"—and since this is many common people of Rome in the audience and the speaker is a great noble, this in itself is a reaching out.

Friends, Romans, countrymen, lend me your ears;

I come to bury Caesar, not to praise him.

The evil that men do lives after them;

The good is oft interred with their bones;

So let it be with Caesar.

I said earlier that when you are presenting your own case, you never want to be negative, even about the opposition. Mark Antony is employing that rule incredibly effectively here: He so over-praises Brutus, so monotonously calls him an honorable man throughout his speech, that the pure contrariness of human nature is beginning to go the other way. The speech is immensely long. It ends in chaos as the crowd so worked up by Mark Antony leaves the rostrum there in the Forum of Rome and goes off to chase down the conspirators to either kill them or drive them out of the city.

It's the rarest thing in the world to actually figure out how to change a crowd's opinion.

There are a number of things to talk about with regard to this speech. One is the use of props. What is Mark Antony using here? He has actually used one thing earlier, the will of Caesar; now he's gone on to the mantel and used the cloak, which Caesar was wearing when he was dying. But then we move on to something very different: He's going to consider not the mantle itself, but the holes that the daggers went through. Keep your focus on your props; keep your focus on showing and telling. Be explicit and clear and not too much on rhetorical tricks.

There is a popular kind of aid to rhetoric now, PowerPoint, in which it's possible to actually put up onto the board behind you your whole speech, or just the outline of it, or just key words. I urge you: Do not do any of these things. Use PowerPoint or slides only for the images to support and reinforce your words. As soon as you put up actual words, the audience's minds shift entirely over into the left part of the brain where all the reasoning is, and they can no longer hear your voice; they can't take in the actual words you're saying in preference to the words they're hypnotically seeing and reading up there on the screen. Don't give them words to read; give them images to see—that's what the props should be.

What kinds of speeches are you likely to make that we can draw out of this Mark Antony speech? One is the tribute—Mark Antony, in this speech, on the behalf of Julius Caesar, is praising Caesar. Certainly one of the areas in which I have been often asked to speak is praise. Sometimes that may be a eulogy at a funeral; sometimes it is a toast at someone's birthday or an anniversary party or an awards ceremony; often it is welcoming a distinguished visitor to Louisville.

We have a Kentucky Author Forum; one time the guest was Madeleine Albright. What would be appropriate for me to say about Madeleine Albright, to say to her, that would induce a sense of praise, link her to high and important things that we all know she was involved in? Our county is called Jefferson County, it was laid out by Thomas Jefferson himself; his statue stands on an imitation of the Liberty Bell down by the courthouse. I told her she was in Jefferson County and Jefferson had been the first secretary of state, the position that she held with such honor for so many years and that she had in a way inherited from Thomas Jefferson. She then had a cue for her speech in that link to Jefferson to talk about him, to talk about how she had read through all of his works, she'd gone back through documents that he had signed as secretary of state. It became very personal to all of us, and I was thankful that I was able to make it personal for her so it wasn't just a reading of her CV.

Whatever it takes whenever you are trying to praise somebody, try to make it personal; try to do what Mark Antony does; try to arouse in your hearers a sense of admiration, a sense of feeling that it is a person that you would like to meet, that you would like to know, and that you definitely admire. ■

Take-Away Points

1. Make a strong beginning.

2. Use props to illustrate and reinforce the points of your speech.

3. Avoid projecting or distributing printed matter while you are speaking.

4. In an argument, be relentless in speaking well of your opponents and courteously allowing for contrary opinions.

5. Pace yourself; move step-by-step in an argument to keep your audience with you.

6. Focus always on concrete points, not on abstractions.

Change Minds and Hearts—Mark Antony

Lecture 11—Transcript

Welcome back. We've been talking about the ways in which you need to engage your audience during a speech, and using different examples of different kinds of speeches as we explore what's important and how the tone of the speech can affect how you want to engage. We were talking last time about these visions, these special speeches that were sharing a personal dream; and there are a few quotes that link the idea of speaking to those dreams and visions that are favorites of mine and I just want to share them with you.

Thoreau, in his book *Walden*, has a wonderful statement: "If one advances confidently in the direction of his dreams, and endeavors to live the life which he has imagined, he will meet with success unexpected in common hours." There's an anonymous quote: "Dreams are the stuff of progress," which I certainly feel in my field, underwater archaeology, everything we do was dreamed by Jules Verne back in the 19th century and technology has scrambled to keep up with him, just as the space program has scrambled to keep up with Jules Verne's idea of getting to the moon. William James, 1902, the brother of the famous American novelist Henry James, was a philosopher of science: "An idea to be suggested must come to an individual with the force of a revelation." I find that fascinating, the idea that even a scientific breakthrough needs to come like a vision from the beyond. Finally, Oliver Wendell Holmes in 1872 about the sort of relationship between the speaker and the listener: "It is the province of knowledge to speak and it is the privilege of wisdom to listen"; where it is the audience that is the source of wisdom and the speaker merely the source of knowledge.

We've been talking about different uses of Aristotle's three kinds of appeals—logos, ethos, pathos—and although our main focus in this lecture is going to be on pathos, on appeals to emotion, and we're going to be focusing on that great speech that Shakespeare wrote for the historical character Mark Antony in Rome in his play *Julius Caesar*, I do want to begin with one other character from Classical history, the Empress Theodora in Byzantium, who is recorded as having given an extraordinary short speech that yes, is an appeal to the emotions, yes is an appeal to reason and logic, but mainly is that ethos that we talked about last time with Martin Luther King, Jr.: that simple situation where you are the message; your own character comes through as the essential argument. The situation is very serious: Rebels are attacking the city of Constantinople, which is the capital of the Byzantine Empire. Empress Theodora is a girl from the streets, a girl who grew up in the circus on the racetrack and was taken out of it by her husband Justinian, a great general; the great general is ready to flee as these rebels approach. Theodora has been present at the council; and as they have decided they will take ship and row away to safety, Theodora, to everyone's amazement, speaks:

> My lords, the situation is too grave for me to obey the custom that a woman does not speak in a council of men. In the most extreme dangers, those who are threatened must consider not customs but the wisest course of action. I believe that to flee would be wrong, even if it should save our lives. All who are born into this world must die, but no monarch should consent to become a fugitive. My lord, if you wish to save yourself, you may do so. We have our treasure, there is the sea, there are our ships. But think, once you have fled to the safety you seek, will you not desire to exchange safety for death? As for me, I hold to the saying that a robe of royal purple makes the noblest of shrouds.

The emperor was not about to flee after that speech. They decided to stay; he, in fact, won a great victory over the rebels and saved his throne, and owed it very much to Theodora, his wife. That is a model of how you are persuasive in your own person; with the firmness, with the clear vision, with allowing for the other person's point of view, and yet arguing very strongly against it.

We're moving now to pathos—to the play of emotions; the appeal to sentiments of sorrow, grief, pity, terror, self interest, all kinds of emotions—that are the third of Aristotle's group of appeals, and we're going to focus on this very famous speech that begins "Friends, Romans, countrymen," maybe the most quoted speech in all the history of theater, from Shakespeare's *Julius Caesar*. The speaker is Mark Antony. In real history, which was written down for us by Plutarch and another historian Dio Cassius—and it's their writings that tell Shakespeare what happened on the occasion when Caesar was assassinated—Brutus, Cassius, Casca, and the other assassins, all friends of Caesar's, now appear to be in control of Rome; but they let Mark Antony, who was a beloved friend of Caesar, speak at the funeral after they have gotten at the crowd first. Caesar's body is there with a bloodstained robe, he's tumbled down the steps of the capitol; the rostrum where the speakers talk in the Forum is there. It's not a podium, it's a platform surrounded by the beaks, the rams, of warships (that's what *rostra* are, they are bronze rams); so it's a victory monument, but it has a nice big platform on the top, and that's what allowed the Roman orators to stride around, to use gestures, to move closer to the audience, go around the platform so they could address all the people and draw near them or draw back in very dramatic ways as if they were on a stage. It's a perfect place for Shakespeare to set his imagination on fire and create a fabulous speech.

Mark Antony is ostensibly, on the surface buying into the idea that the assassination of Caesar was necessary, that Caesar was ambitious to become a monarch or a tyrant, and that what the conspirators did was just. In his heart, he is wanting to work on the emotions of the crowd, who've been convinced by the previous speeches of Brutus and the others that what was done was just; he wants to bring them over to a sense of outrage, he wants to turn the crowd against Brutus and the other conspirators. I consider this to be the hardest thing in all of public speaking, although in many books written about the subject you will hear about the persuasive speech that changes people's minds. I haven't heard many of those speeches; I'm not sure I've ever given one myself except at one zoning board meeting and I'll be glad to share that with you later. Most people are really only reinforced in their original opinions by a speech; they can be stirred up to higher levels of enthusiasm or depressed to lower levels of grief that they already felt, or they can be moved from neutral people sitting in the middle on an issue one way or the other. It's the rarest thing in the world to actually figure out how to change a crowd's opinion. These are Shakespeare's words, remember—we don't know exactly what the original Mark Antony said—but Shakespeare has given us a model on how to work on people's emotions to change their fundamental attitude to a situation.

We start with the strongest beginning of any speech I know. It immediately grabs the attention; it identifies the speaker with the audience by calling them "friends"—and since this is many common people of Rome in the audience and the speaker is a great noble, this in itself is a reaching out, a great indulgent form of getting onto the audience's level; it's unforgettable, as is much of the speech. Let's just go ahead and hear it now:

> Friends, Romans, countrymen, lend me your ears;
> I come to bury Caesar, not to praise him.
> The evil that men do lives after them;
> The good is oft interred with their bones;
> So let it be with Caesar. The noble Brutus
> Hath told you Caesar was ambitious:
> If it were so, it was a grievous fault,
> And grievously hath Caesar answer'd it.
> Here, under leave of Brutus and the rest—
> For Brutus is an honourable man;
> So are they all, all honourable men—
> Come I to speak in Caesar's funeral.
> He was my friend, faithful and just to me:
> But Brutus says he was ambitious;
> And Brutus is an honourable man.
> He hath brought many captives home to Rome
> Whose ransoms did the general coffers fill:
> Did this in Caesar seem ambitious?
> When that the poor have cried, Caesar hath wept:
> Ambition should be made of sterner stuff:
> Yet Brutus says he was ambitious; …
> And, sure, he is an honourable man.
> I speak not to disprove what Brutus spoke,
> But here I am to speak what I do know.
> You all did love him once, not without cause:
> What cause withholds you then, to mourn for him?
> O judgment! thou art fled to brutish beasts,
> And men have lost their reason. Bear with me;
> My heart is in the coffin there with Caesar,
> And I must pause till it come back to me.

We're not at an ending, we're at a place where Mark Antony breaks off to simulate weeping, and the crowd gets to mutter and murmur. I said earlier that when you are presenting your own case, you never want to be negative, even about the opposition. Mark Antony is employing that rule incredibly effectively here: He is so over-praising Brutus, so monotonously calling him an honorable man, that the pure contrariness of human nature is beginning to go the other way. I'd also like you to notice this does not have a tripartite structure; we have no idea where we are in his speech—introduction, middle, end, who knows?—and his audience is being jerked around by his variations in tone, those things I told you not to do, about changing abruptly from one tone to another. Mark Antony is a master of this here: He is working on their sympathies by seeming like he's being muzzled by this command and forced to say things he doesn't want to say, suddenly erupting in great emotion; earlier saying, "Oh, the evil that men do lives after them; the good is oft interred with their bones; so let it be with Caesar," very resigned, and then he's a firebrand by the end. This keeps them off balance; this is preparing you for the fact that in this state of uneasiness and uncertainty, he's going to be able to push them the way he wants them to go. It's a masterful psychological study on Shakespeare's part, and these are lessons that any of us could use if we're up against a crowd that needs to be gotten off balance and needs to be moved in the direction that we would like to see them make their choice.

After all of their talk and their beginning to doubt—Shakespeare has a number of citizens speaking to each other—we're suddenly back with Mark Antony:

> If you have tears, prepare to shed them now.
> You all do know this mantle: I remember
> The first time ever Caesar put it on;
> 'Twas on a summer's evening, in his tent,
> That day he overcame the Nervii:
> Look, in this place ran Cassius' dagger through:
> See what a rent the envious Casca made:
> Through this the well-beloved Brutus stabb'd;
> And as he pluck'd his cursed steel away,
> Mark how the blood of Caesar follow'd it,
> As rushing out of doors, to be resolved

If Brutus so unkindly knock'd, or no;
For Brutus, as you know, was Caesar's angel:
Judge, O you gods, how dearly Caesar loved him!
This was the most unkindest cut of all; …

I'm not going to go on with the speech, it's immensely long. It ends in chaos as the crowd so worked up by Mark Antony leave the rostrum there in the Forum of Rome and go off to chase down the conspirators to either kill them or drive them out of the city; and Mark Antony is left very pleased with himself on the rostrum. All of his emotion is a show, although he does have fondness for the dead Caesar and that's genuine, but nothing like what he's imitating here.

We have a number of things to talk about. One is the use of props; we haven't really considered that too much. We've been talking about you, yourself as your own prop with your gestures, with your movements on the platform, with your expression of your face, your eye contact; all of these things make the visual side of your presentation. But it's often very important to incorporate these props. I mentioned my own experience with the zoning board: I had to offer a speech trying to prevent the clear cutting of trees on a slope below my house, and I was aware that the slope was made up of a crumbly shale, it was really just sort of layers of mud that had become a soft stone; so I carried in some of this shale, wet it down, passed it around to the members of the zoning board so they could feel that this stuff, as soon as it was exposed by the cutting of the trees, would start to wash away in the rains. We won the case; I'd like to think partly because of the tactile impression of that prop.

What is Mark Antony using here? He's actually used another one earlier, the will of Caesar; now he's gone on to the mantel, the cloak, which Caesar was wearing when he was dying, that beautiful touch of remembering the summer evening when Caesar first put it on and that he was in the tent. "Oh, it was that day when he defeated the Nervii," the tribe that were enemies of Rome, harping on all of his services to the people. But then we move on to something very different: He's going to consider not the mantle itself, but the holes that the daggers went through. He cannot possibly know which hole went with which dagger, he wasn't there; but he's willing to use his own imagination to personify those holes, to make them speak like bloody mouths, the blood of Caesar was all around them. That final thing, "This was the most unkindest cut of all," what a resonant line, what a powerful thing; and that double superlative—which defines the grammarians—"most unkindest" really seems to hit home. He goes a little off track—it's hard to say this of Shakespeare—but that business of how the blood of Caesar rushed out after the steel went in as if coming out of a door to see who had knocked on it, I think that's a bit of Elizabethan fancy we could have done without. Keep your focus on your props; keep your focus on showing, telling, be explicit and clear and not too much on rhetorical tricks. I think with a second edit Shakespeare might have pulled that pair of lines there.

At any rate, props are important; props are going to be something that can help make the emotional force of your appeal even stronger. Of course, it can also help in the logos, in the reasoning if you can show something: When I'm archaeologically speaking in my classes I will try to show archaeological artifacts in order to make the points. There's always a question: Do you want to hand things around in class? Sometimes that distracts from the words; and this point of distraction with props and with visual aids is very important. There is a popular kind of aid to rhetoric now, PowerPoint, in which it's possible to actually throw up onto the board behind you your whole speech, or just the outline of it, or just key words. I urge you: Do not do any of these things. Use PowerPoint, use slides only for the images to support and reinforce your words. As soon as you put up actual words, the audiences' minds shift entirely over into the left part of the brain where all the reasoning is—the logic, the cerebral processing and analysis—and they can no longer hear your voice; they can't take in the actual words you're saying in preference to the words they're hypnotically seeing and reading up there on the board or on the screen. Don't give them words to read; give them images to see, give them objects to look at, that's what the props should be.

Mark Antony is a genius at manipulation. Let's follow just a little bit more of how he turns this into an emotional rollercoaster. First of all, he is managing his tone throughout. He started low, he started quiet; in spite of the clarion call of "Friends, Romans, countrymen," once he gets into his speech, the second line—"I come to bury Caesar, not to praise him."—What could be more level, more smooth, more modest in tone than that? It gives no inclination of where he's going; it gives him a low place to begin so he can shoot off by the end of the speech into extremes of emotion. Again, you'll often read, "Make your beginning strong." Make your call to attention clear. The beginning should simply give you a breathing space from which to move, a low point, a sort of initial standing place; and it's the end of the speech that really needs to be worked on, and we're going to see that next time when we talk about "The Gettysburg Address" and Lincoln. I am not of the school that thinks that you are sunk if you can't grab people by the throat with your opening words. I think that the important thing in the opening words is right what Mark Antony does: He's probably spoken here before, but he wants to hear his own voice and he wants to get their attention; by declaiming "Friends, Romans, countrymen, lend me your ears," he's had a chance to focus their eyes on him and to get a sound of his own voice coming back to him, so he's judged the space and he knows now how to be comfortable speaking in it. But then he's getting off to a very modest start; you can follow his example very well.

We are in a world here of using these different rhetorical devices that I think calls up some interesting reflections about how this speech has been used by different people and what it's meant to different people. I'd like you remember back to Jane Austen's *Mansfield Park*—which I quoted in our second lecture when we were talking about control of body language and so on—you'll remember the two young Bertram brothers, Tom and Edmund, had been required by their father, so that they would learn to speak well as boys, to memorize different speeches and declaim them to their father after they had memorized them; and the result was that Tom Bertram is able to name this speech as one of the ones he'd memorized, that he had spent one of his vacations, his holidays, back home declaiming the death of Julius Caesar to his father.

I also have a dear friend who became very interested in this speech as the result of something that happened to her in school. She was a very shy girl and she had a serious crisis in self-confidence as well; she was not only shy with other people, she was unsure of herself. The class was given an assignment: Pick a speech, memorize it, and declaim it to the class. She was memorizing and memorizing this very "Friends, Romans, countrymen" speech; and as she was at home, her family got to hear it and her mother said to her at one point, "I don't think you're really putting much into this. The emotion of the speech is not coming across. How would you really make them pay attention? How would you get them excited?" The young girl, then about 12, said, "Well, I guess I might stand on a chair." "Then why don't you try it that way?" She stood on the chair, she really declaimed it, she put her heart and soul in it, her mother applauded and told her, "You should do it just that way in class." When she got to school the next day and it was her turn—all the others had simply stood up at their places—she stood on her chair just as Mark Antony would have stood on the speaker's rostrum in the Forum, she declaimed the speech, and at the end there was a moment of complete shocked silence (many in the class had never heard her voice) and then a standing ovation. Shakespeare does a lot, public speaking can do a lot, to help a person get over shyness, to help them see what they can be in the world using their own voice, using their own ideas.

What kinds of speeches are you likely to make that we can kind of draw out of this Mark Antony speech? One is the tribute—I think we need to always consider as we're going over the whole field of public speaking, of the different situations in which you're going to have to do it—Mark Antony, in this speech, on the behalf of Julius Caesar, is praising Caesar. He's doing exactly what he said he wouldn't do when he first walked on—"I come to bury Caesar, not to praise him."—that's total falsehood; he's praising him all the way through, first subtly and then very overtly. Certainly one of the areas in which I have been often asked to speak is praise. Sometimes that may be a eulogy at a funeral; sometimes it is a toast at someone's birthday or an anniversary party or an awards ceremony; often it is welcoming a distinguished visitor to Louisville and praising them, but also making the crowd feel that this is a very grand and special occasion that these folks have come to our city.

We have a Kentucky Author Forum; one time the guest was Madeleine Albright. What would be appropriate for me to say about Madeleine Albright, to say to her, that would induce a sense of praise, link her to high and important things that we all know she was involved in? Our county is called Jefferson County, it was laid out by Thomas Jefferson himself, his statue stands on an imitation of the Liberty Bell down by the courthouse; and so she didn't know this. I told her, she was in Jefferson County and Jefferson had been the first Secretary of State, the position that she held with such honor for so many years and that she had in a way inherited from Thomas Jefferson. She then had a cue for her speech in that link to Jefferson to talk about him, to talk about how she had read through all of his works, she'd gone back through documents that he had signed as Secretary of State. It became very personal to all of us, and I was thankful that I was able to make it personal for her so it wasn't just a reading of the CV. I think if you'll read through the speech on your own again you'll see how Mark Antony is careful to personalize all the important facts about Caesar in the areas that we didn't go into: Caesar's love for the poor, his leaving them things in his will (the reading of the will itself turns into quite a scene); all of this is something important for you to consider as you are thinking about how to personalize praise for someone.

One more from these introductions: I was asked to introduce Sandra Day O'Connor; I read up on her and discovered she doesn't like to be praised. She's a no-nonsense person who grew up on a ranch down in the southwest and she finds praise kind of offensive. So, again, I looked for a contact between her life and our community. It so happens that my hometown of New Albany, Indiana had been the hometown of a Supreme Court Justice; his name was Sherman Minton, he had been friends with my grandparents. I also heard that she had run-ins with rattlesnakes, and so on, on her ranch, and she was interested and accustomed to the company of dangerous snakes. This funny story about Sherman Minton that's told in our community, was told to me by my grandmother who was there for the big event: He had invited, after he became Supreme Court Justice, all of the local folks there in New Albany to a big dinner at his house to meet some people from Washington; it was going to be a really elegant affair. On the morning of the big dinner he went down to the basement and told his son, young Sherman, to get rid of all of his snakes and his collection of reptiles that he'd brought up from the woods. Young Sherman went around, emptied all the cages, but the biggest cage was already empty. This six-foot black snake had gotten loose into the house, and the whole family had to spend the day tearing the place apart trying to find the black snake. They couldn't find it, the guests arrived; it was the strangest dinner in living memory according to my grandmother. The Chief Justice and his wife seemed paralyzed, they couldn't finish a sentence; they were obviously terrified the black snake was going to come out from under a sofa or drop from a chandelier. Finally, the guests left and everything seemed fine, they were sure the snake had gotten away just unseen into the woods, when Mrs. Minton lifted the roses out of the big bowl that had been sitting in the middle of the formal dinner table the entire time and began to scream and scream, and the justice Sherman Minton ran over to see what was wrong, there was the black snake coiled up inside that bowl.

It got a laugh at the dinner, she laughed, too (Sandra Day O'Connor), she responded with many herpetological jokes and stories of her own; but it was a way, I felt, of praising her, of showing that we in Louisville and in New Albany knew her background, wanted to match the kind of things that she would be interested in, wanted to meet her on her own ground rather than simply giving the kind of platitudes that you would find in a CV or an online resume. Whatever it takes whenever you are trying to praise somebody, try to make it personal; try to do what Mark Antony does; try to arouse in your hearers a sense of admiration, a sense of feeling that it is a person that you would like to meet, would like to know, and that you definitely admire.

Now we're going to consider the lessons that we get out of Mark Antony's address to those Romans: First, make a strong beginning; "Friends, Romans, countrymen, lend me your ears" is a great way to start. Second, use props to illustrate and reinforce the points of your speech. Anything that you can hold up and show makes a very powerful effect. But, avoid projecting or distributing printed matter while you are speaking; don't have any words up on the screen, the brains of your listeners will immediately latch onto those printed words, they'll be distracted from your own voice. We have a few other things we need to remember from this wonderful speech by Shakespeare: In an argument, be relentless in speaking well of your opponents, and courteously allowing for contrary opinions. Your audience may actually shift to your opinion based on your over-praising of the opposition. Pace yourself; move step by step in an argument to keep your audience with you. Even though Mark Antony is jerking the crowd around point to point emotionally, the actual flow of his movement from pretending not to praise Caesar to praising him unreservedly is very carefully judged. Finally, focus always on concrete points, not on abstractions. The holding up of the bloody mantle and the showing of the holes that were torn by the knives of the assassins spoke more loudly in itself than any amount of words from Mark Antony.

Call for Positive Action—Lincoln at Gettysburg

Lecture 12

We talked last time about Mark Antony and his surprising way of keeping his audience off balance; that's a good thing to do, you never want the audience to settle into complacency and feel they know exactly what's coming. If you've had a standard format for a speech or if you've been setting a pattern, break it now and then just to make sure they're still listening.

Our featured speech in this lecture is Lincoln's Gettysburg Address, certainly my candidate for the greatest speech ever written. Here are some lessons to keep in mind as we examine this and other great speeches: First, incorporate the element of surprise through unexpected elements in your speech, such as breaks in established patterns or conventional contents. Second, employ simple language and short words. Third, repeat important words, many times if necessary, to reinforce your message. Next, include a clear call for action in your speech near the end; let your audience know what you want them to do or think or feel. Finally, craft the strongest possible ending.

Library of Congress, Prints & Photographs Division, LC-DIG-ppmsca-19241.

Abraham Lincoln ended the Gettysburg Address with the call to reunite the country.

I'd like to begin with that part of a speech that we have so far neglected, but which is one of the most important of all: the ending. No part of a speech can have a greater impact on the audience's overall impression than the last words they hear from you, and that's why you must be so careful in crafting the strongest possible ending for any public address that you make. Please, spend a lot of time knowing exactly where you're going in the speech, and when you get there, drive that message home. Not only do the words need to be strong, you need to deliver them strongly. If you've been reading your speech up to that point, memorize the end so you can lift your head. When you get there, lift your head, fix the audience with a (we hope) engaging gaze, and deliver that peroration in a way that really connects with them. You will be rewarded, believe me, by a very healthy round of applause. What you must do then is be silent and give them time to applaud. Too many speakers come to the end of their speech and then ruin the entire effect with an offhand remark.

Spend a lot of time knowing exactly where you're going in the speech, and when you get there, drive that message home.

Abraham Lincoln was asked in 1863, a few days after the terrible battle at Gettysburg, to add to the occasion not the primary eulogy speech itself, but a few remarks. Lincoln obviously felt that this was going to be one of the important moments of his presidency. This was one of the greatest battles in American history in terms of the scale, it was a great turning point in the war; Lincoln felt he must be the equal of the occasion itself. The myth that he wrote it down, scribbling on the back of an envelope on the train from Washington out into the Pennsylvania countryside is just that: a myth. He did not; many sketches have been found of that speech, and it's known that he worked for at least two weeks to perfect it. To go on and on at great length, to have no limits to the diversions and digressions you can go into, any ready speaker can fill the hours of talk. But when you have to boil down your meaning to just a few minutes—and the Gettysburg Address is only 270 words and only takes about three minutes to deliver—that is the supreme challenge. Here is the speech in its entirety:

> Fellow countrymen. Four score and seven years ago our fathers brought forth, upon this continent, a new nation, conceived in Liberty, and dedicated to the proposition that all men are created equal.

> Now we are engaged in a great civil war, testing whether that nation, or any nation so conceived, and so dedicated, can long endure. We are met here on a great battlefield of that war. We have come to dedicate a portion of it as a final resting place for those who here gave their lives that that nation might live. It is altogether fitting and proper that we should do this.
>
> But in a larger sense we can not dedicate—we can not consecrate—we can not hallow this ground. The brave men, living and dead, who struggled, here, have consecrated it far above our poor power to add or detract. The world will little note, nor long remember, what we say here, but can never forget what they did here.
>
> It is for us, the living, rather to be dedicated here to the unfinished work which they who fought here have, thus far, so nobly advanced. It is rather for us to be here dedicated to the great task remaining before us—that from these honored dead we take increased devotion to that cause for which they gave the last full measure of devotion—that we here highly resolve that these dead shall not have died in vain; that this nation under God shall have a new birth of freedom; and that government of the people, by the people, for the people, shall not perish from the earth.

Note that he never mentions the enemy, he doesn't mention the situations of the war, it's on some higher plane; not an abstraction exactly, but we're up way high. How many times does he use the word "dedication" in here? Six times in this short speech. This is his focus, dedication. They came here to dedicate a cemetery. But it's because he asked the living to do something about it—not just to reflect on it, not just to bear witness to it—that this speech is the extraordinarily great speech that it is.

Let's look at just a few of the things that make it so remarkable. One is the simplicity of the language: Most of his words are one-syllable words. Note the biblical echoes: He's tying what happened here into the whole of world history and of religious history. "Four score and seven years ago"—he's after a certain tone, a certain power in the language. We get another final lesson from this, and it comes from the set of words he uses most often: "we," "us," "our"—14 times in this speech. He never says "I"; he never says "you"; it's always "we." That's an ideal for us all to follow as speakers; to establish a complete unity with our audience. If we can remember to do that, we will have taken one little step along the road that Lincoln wanted us to follow of being inspired by these men's lives. ■

Take-Away Points

1. Create empathy between yourself and your listeners with your words.

2. Combine ethos (the idea of personality) and pathos (the idea of healing), and shift the focus of your speech from "I" or "you" to "we."

Call for Positive Action—Lincoln at Gettysburg

Lecture 12—Transcript

Welcome back to the 12th and the final lecture in our course on public speaking. I have enjoyed this long journey with all of its twists and turns and varied landscape, I hope you've been enjoying it, too; and I look forward to the time when I may be sitting down in an audience and realize that it's you up there on the podium delivering a speech that I expect to enjoy very much.

We talked last time about Mark Antony and his surprising way of keeping his audience off balance; that's a good thing to do, you never want the audience to settle into complacency and feel they know exactly what's coming. If you've had a standard format for a speech or if you've been setting a pattern, break it now and then just to make sure they're still listening. We're going to do that now. We've been having our lessons drawn from our speeches, drawn from our guest professors; we've been having those lessons come at the end of the talk, we are now going to break the pattern, take you by surprise: lessons first, speech later.

Here we go: Our featured speech today is Lincoln's "Gettysburg Address," certainly my candidate for the greatest speech ever written. I'd like you to think as we are working our way through some other speakers and some other ideas towards that great "Gettysburg Address" of these following lessons: First, incorporate the element of surprise through unexpected elements in your speech, such as breaks in established patterns or conventional contents. Second, employ simple language and short words whenever you speak in public. Third, repeat important words, many times if necessary, to reinforce your message. Next, include a clear call for action in your speech near the end; let your audience know what you want them to do or think or feel. Finally, appropriately, craft the strongest possible ending. There's actually one more lesson, but I'm saving it for the very end; we will hear the speech, I hope you will be struck by a very unusual thing that Lincoln does all the way through that speech. We will talk about it at the very end because for me it's one of the prime messages that Lincoln is sending us as we review the words of that unforgettable address.

I'd like to begin today with that part of a speech that we have so far neglected, but which is one of the most important of all: the ending. The "Gettysburg Address" has a great ending, so do a number of other speeches; but, of course, we've also seen a couple where, in my opinion, the speaker has run off the rails and done something at the ending to weaken the effect of the entire speech. No part of the speech can have a greater impact on the audience's overall impression than the last words they hear from you; and that's why you must be so careful in crafting the strongest possible ending for any public address that you make. I'd like you to consider a metaphor or simile from the world of sports: In diving—which I watch when the Olympics are on the television—I notice that the judges are always obsessed with the way the feet of the diver enter the water. What seems like an extraordinarily difficult dive, perfectly performed, can receive huge demerits in the scoring if the feet flopped over, if there's a big splash, if they're not perfectly vertical, descending without a ripple into the swimming pool. That's the finish, that's like the end of the speech; that's what your audience is going to remember most. As I said last time when we talked about beginnings—and, of course, Mark Antony gives us a wonderful beginning, "Friends, Romans, countrymen, lend me your ears"—I don't care what the books say, beginnings don't matter so much. It's fine to ease your way in; it's fine to get the sense of the hall with a few casual remarks and thanks to the audience and to the person who has just introduced you. Endings aren't like that; endings must be strong. Endings are more important for their sort of leverage on the audience's reaction, as I just said, than any other single part of the speech. Please, spend a lot of time knowing exactly where you're going in the speech, and when you get there drive that message home.

Let's look at what I consider to be an ending on a par with the beautiful ending that Lincoln contrived for the "Gettysburg Address." This is from a speech by Nelson Mandela. The year is 1964. He's on trial for fighting against the apartheid system, and he is justifying what he's done and taking advantage of the trial—much as Gandhi did back in the 1920s—the trial itself is serving as a platform for him to state his beliefs and his ideals and his motives. He really spent a lot of time on this ending; and it was so much still in his mind that 26 years later, when he was finally released from Prison in 1990, on being freed and giving a speech then he used this ending as the close of that speech, and I think you will understand why.

> I have fought against white domination, and I have fought against black domination. I have cherished the ideal of a democratic and free society in which all persons live together in harmony and with equal opportunities. It is an ideal which I hope to live for and to achieve. But if needs be, it is an ideal for which I am prepared to die.

Without a single rhetorical flourish, image, piece of vivid language, Nelson Mandela has established a sense of himself in those words of his integrity, of his devotion to a cause, of his determination even to die for the cause if necessary. That must have left the courtroom, I hope, in awe of that giant of a character that was before them. The sincerity of it is very strong, and the turn at the end, it doesn't quite go where you think it's going to, that slight element of surprise that I mentioned as being important: "It is an ideal which I hope to live for and to achieve" but then, "But if needs be, it is an ideal for which I am prepared to die." That comes like the blow of a hammer at the end of that speech; awed, stunned silence would be the only appropriate reaction to follow those words. You may not want to induce such an extraordinary response in your audience, but you do need to think about the end of your speech.

I would like you to think back to that specific other speech we talked about where the ending was weakened because it went on one sentence too long, and that was Susan B. Anthony, speaking for women's suffrage. She had a beautiful final sentence on everything that women's suffrage meant to her, the importance of this injustice being redressed, and then could not stop herself and added a sentence comparing women's suffrage to the rights that had been extended to Negroes by law after the Civil War. That's where she stopped; the focus had suddenly shifted. It doesn't matter to what other object she shifted it; she was wrong to move the audience's attention at the very end away from the focus of her speech. For Nelson Mandela, that statement is the focus of the speech; to live or to die for the ideals, that says it all. Your final speech should be a reaffirmation of your most important point; that is the last place in a speech that you want to bring up a digression, a diversion of interest, a detail that doesn't quite fit in but seemed interesting to you. You must be ruthless and rigorous in plotting out how your speech will end so that it ends at its moment of greatest strength and not sort of on an off beat or a second step that weakens the effect of the whole.

There are some other points to remember when you're finishing a speech: Not only do the words need to be strong, you need to deliver them strongly. If you've been reading your speech up to that point, please memorize the very ending so you can lift your head. Remember, I'm not after you if you have to read from a script; it may be a way station, it may be something you'll need to do all your life, but for the last lines, memorize them so when you see them coming you lift your head, you fix the audience with a (we hope) engaging gaze and you deliver that peroration, that finale, in a way that really connects with them, really grabs them. It's very important. You will be rewarded, believe me, by a very healthy round of applause. What you must do, also, is give them time to applause. I can't tell you how many speakers I've listened to who come to the end of their speech and then ruin the entire effect with an offhand remark.

Let's go on to one of our next speakers to hear from today, I'll just read the end of his speech. This is Pericles of Athens. What would it have been like if he had ended his eulogy on the young men of Athens who had been killed in combat during the first year of the Peloponnesian War if he had ended it this way?

> In foreign lands there dwells also an unwritten memorial of them, graven not on stone but in the hearts of men. Make them your examples. Do I hear any questions?

It's not good; it's not even good in a simple lecture in a classroom. There may be questions, there may be not, but you have killed the effect of your speech by running off into an offhand comment or question or asking if you have enough time to talk some more, anything like that. The final moment of your speech needs to be like those divers' feet, disappearing straight down into the water, not a ripple behind: a moment of silence, the applause breaks out. Believe me, it's a good feeling, not just for you; do this for the audience. They've spent anywhere up to an hour—in some of my cases of long classes two and a half hours—listening to you; they deserve the chance to communicate back with their applause, to reaffirm for themselves that this was an occasion that mattered. Please do them that courtesy: Finish strong, be silent; never ask if there are any questions. If there are any, they'll raise their hands; or the people who've organized it will step up onto the platform with you and say, "I'm sure that our speaker will be glad to take some questions," and, of course, you will be. That's the way it should all end, be careful: Endings are more important in public speaking than beginnings.

There's another point I mentioned in our lessons, and that's this question of trying to find a way to let the public know, let the people who are listening to you know, what you want them to do. What's the message? You're guiding them to something. Don't simply give a string of facts and let them lie out there inertly. One of the beautiful examples of this I know is a famous speech by the Buddha, Gautama Siddhartha, that young Indian prince born in what is today Tibet who way back around 500 B.C. created one of the world's great religions. He obviously did not do a lot of public oratory; his was a quiet seeking of a true path through life and through some withdrawal from society in many ways. But he did leave a beautiful mediation, a record of a meditation, that he performed and then remembered all of his life, one that happened while he was sitting under a bodhi tree at a place called Bodh Gaya; there's a big shrine there now, there's even a big tree growing that is said to be a descendent of the original, there's a big wall around the place. Pilgrims come and know they're at the place where Gautama Siddhartha acquired enlightenment. He wants to share the enlightenment with you, and he wants to feel that you are one of those whose eyes are not so covered with dust, but that you will hear the words, you will understand, and you will follow the way. He is giving a gentle version of his vision, giving you a gentle version of his experience of enlightenment as he sees these truths, and then presenting them to you with the idea that now you will have heard and you will do likewise.

Let me explain a few things: He's going to refer to the Four Noble Truths; they all involve suffering. The first noble truth is, "To exist is to suffer." The second noble truth is that "Suffering comes from desire and craving for the things of this world." The third noble truth: "Suffering can end when you renounce desire and craving." Finally, "You can achieve that end by following the Eightfold Path"; these are eight qualities from perfect understanding all the way to perfect contemplation. In doing this, you achieve release from karma, and that is the burden on you from past lives in that Indian system of reincarnation. That's what's behind what you're going to hear. Here is Buddha giving his vision, but steering all of his listeners towards making a choice; making it very clear what he wants them to do, which path he hopes they will take:

> Oh my disciples. So long as certain knowledge and clear vision of the Four Noble Truths was denied to me, I felt uncertain about achieving the supreme enlightenment, which is the highest thing in this world of celestial beings, bad spirits and gods, ascetics and holy men, immortals and mortals. But when I felt I had achieved complete knowledge and insight into the Four Noble Truths, I immediately felt sure that I had reached Supreme Enlightenment, and I found out that deepest truth, so hard to see, so hard to comprehend, yet peace-giving and heavenly that you cannot reach by reason alone and which can be seen only by those who have attained wisdom. But the world is given over to pleasures of the senses. It is obsessed by pleasure, seduced by pleasure, charmed by pleasure. In truth, such worldly beings can hardly comprehend the law of conditionality and the dependent origin of all things. Likewise, they cannot understand the end of all forms, the liberation from previous lives, the fading away of desire, detaching from the world, perishing from the world, nirvana. But there are those whose eyes are blinded only a little by earthly dust; they will know the truth.

To all of the disciples sitting around him, that was a clarion call: We are the ones whose eyes are only a little clouded by the dust; we are the ones who will see the truth; we are the ones who will follow our master into this perfect enlightenment that he has so beautifully described. I can't forbear pointing out that even in India in 500 B.C., the Buddha is thinking in threes as he describes the ways pleasures attack people with obsessions, with seductions, with charms; those three clauses are very charming in themselves, and maybe they were meant to be.

Let's look at this issue of funeral eulogies as an example of a kind of speech where you might not expect a call to action. Lincoln's "Gettysburg Address" is a eulogy, is a clear call to an action or a response, a way to think or feel differently afterwards. Funeral eulogies can be very difficult, they can often dissolve in tears—I've wept through them myself—you need to find something for people to go away with, as you do in any speech; but especially here, especially when you're mourning or grieving for a dead one and you want to offer hope, you want to in some cases offer laughter even, to turn the grief around, to keep it at bay, to set the living back on their feet and start them off on a new path. Let's go back to about the same time when Buddha was writing; we're in the fifth century B.C., but we're in Athens, Greece, and that man I invoked a moment earlier in a very rude way by ending his phrases with a question that he didn't ask. Pericles of Athens, the great general, the great leader of the Athenians, has been asked by the people to read the funeral oration for their honored dead after a year's fighting, the first year of the Peloponnesian War with the Spartans. To be asked to read that funeral oration was a supreme honor for an Athenian citizen. The state funeral ground was on a sacred way stretching out from the city gates toward the Academy where the philosophers taught, and there those who had died in the service of their country would all be laid together. It was the Athenian Arlington.

From the middle part of his speech, I take the passage where Pericles gives them, and in an echo gives us, a sense of what to do about our grief at a funeral, especially of those who've died young. First, he starts by focusing on his listeners, and what they should feel about the city that these young men died for.

> I would have you day by day fix your eyes upon the greatness of Athens, until you become filled with the love of her; and when you are impressed by the spectacle of her glory, reflect that this empire has been acquired by men who knew their duty and had the courage to do it ... the whole earth is the sepulcher of famous men; not only are they commemorated by columns and inscriptions in their own country, but in foreign lands there dwells also an unwritten memorial of them, graven not on stone but in the hearts of men. Make them your examples.

With that final sentence, "Make them your examples," Pericles has turned his speech from a speech of mourning into a speech of motivation, of exhortation. This is something for you to do, to think, to feel, that they are my new examples, I shall follow in their path; and then unspoken by Pericles is the corollary, "Thus they will not have lived in vain. They will have made a difference to this world. By my own actions, I can ensure that it will happen."

Pericles's "Funeral Oration" was one of the many speeches of antiquity that was studied by young Abraham Lincoln. He knew these words, he knew the words of the great Roman authors; he studied Scott's *Lessons in Elocution*, which was a big encyclopedia of excerpts from plays, from essays, from famous speeches of the past; all of his knowledge of those earlier speakers came together when he was asked in 1863, a few days after the terrible battle at Gettysburg—which, although a Union victory, was disastrous in terms of the thousands who were lost there—he was asked to add to the occasion not the primary eulogy speech itself, but a few remarks.

Lincoln obviously felt that this was going to be one of the important moments of his presidency. This was one of the greatest battles in American history in terms of the scale, it was a great turning point in the war; Lincoln felt he must be the equal of the occasion itself. The myth that he wrote it down, scribbling on the back of an envelope on the train from Washington out into the Pennsylvania countryside is just that: a myth. I'm sorry to say the myth was promulgated by his own son after Lincoln's death. The son was nowhere near Lincoln at the time when this was done; who knows, it may have been from an offhand joke on the part of his father, who was always humble and who might have told the boy, when hearing praises of the "Gettysburg Address," "Ah, I scribbled it out on the train." He did not; many sketches have been found of that speech, it's known that he worked for at least two weeks to perfect it. It goes along with an observation that Lincoln once made: A five minute address is very hard to create; as for a two-hour oration, as he once said, "I'm ready now." To go on and on at great length, to have no limits to the diversions and digressions you can go into, any ready speaker can fill the hours of talk. But when you have to boil down your meaning to just a few minutes—and the "Gettysburg Address" is only 270 words and only takes about three minutes to deliver—that is the supreme challenge. As I said earlier, remember he was able to do this very short speech because the work of the day had been done by Edward Everett, a great speaker who wrote and delivered a two-hour funeral eulogy about the men, talking about them, talking about their sacrifice. Lincoln did not want to sound those same notes in summary in his; he came up with something different.

You'll sometimes hear that at the end of the "Gettysburg Address" the crowd was not impressed; it's true that some newspapers later, having only the texts of the two speeches—the two-hour oration by Everett and then Lincoln's very short remarks—concluded that Lincoln had not done enough for the occasion. But we have it on the testimony of eyewitnesses that after Edward Everett's oration ended, they all sang a hymn together, and then people were actually beginning to disperse a bit during the hymn. Lincoln stood up, his commanding voice drew them back to the platform, and in those short three minutes he was interrupted five times by cheering. That's not the way this speech is normally read; I'm going to try to give it to you with some of that feel in mind: that this is a rallying cry; that he's trying to say what we should do about this, not simply what we should feel about it.

> Fellow countrymen. Four score and seven years ago our fathers brought forth, upon this continent, a new nation, conceived in Liberty, and dedicated to the proposition that all men are created equal.
>
> Now we are engaged in a great civil war, testing whether that nation, or any nation so conceived, and so dedicated, can long endure. We are met here on a great battlefield of that war. We have come to dedicate a portion of it as a final resting place for those who here gave their lives that that nation might live. It is altogether fitting and proper that we should do this.
>
> But in a larger sense we can not dedicate—we can not consecrate—we can not hallow this ground. The brave men, living and dead, who struggled, here, have consecrated it far above our poor power to add or detract. The world will little note, nor long remember, what we say here, but can never forget what they did here.
>
> It is for us, the living, rather to be dedicated here to the unfinished work which they who fought here have, thus far, so nobly advanced. It is rather for us to be here dedicated to the great task remaining

> before us—that from these honored dead we take increased devotion to that cause for which they gave the last full measure of devotion—that we here highly resolve that these dead shall not have died in vain; that this nation under God shall have a new birth of freedom; and that government of the people, by the people, for the people, shall not perish from the earth.

You know that they cheered; you know that they cheered because he had given them a sense that this all mattered. Note that he never mentions the enemy, he doesn't mention the situations of the war, it's on some higher plane; not an abstraction exactly, but we're up way high. Remember Thomas Jefferson at his inaugural address talking about the high ground on which a president stood to see that which others could not; Lincoln's up there, he takes his listeners up there with him and he makes sure that they are going to understand the full importance of what they do. After this ceremony, you can't do anything for the dead, you're not even worthy to do anything to the dead or for the dead; it's for the dead to inspire us. How many times does he use the word "dedication" in here? Six times in this short speech. This is his focus, dedication. They came here to dedicate a cemetery. It's still there, people still visit it; people still feel moved by the presence of that grief all around them and by the words of Lincoln ringing in their ears. But it's because he asked the living to do something about it; not just to reflect on it, not just to bear witness to it, but to do something that this speech is the extraordinarily great speech that it is.

Let's look at just a few of the things that make it so remarkable. One is the simplicity of the language: Most of his words are one-syllable words; this has often been remarked on. Note the biblical echoes: He's tying what happened here into the whole of world history and of religious history. "Four score and seven years ago"; "87 years ago" would have done it, but he's after a certain tone, a certain power in the language. Finally, I promised you that you were going to get a final lesson from this, and it comes from the set of words he uses most often: "we," "us," "our" 14 times in this speech. He never says "I," he never says "you," it's always "we." That's an ideal for us all to follow as speakers; to establish a complete unity with our audience.

So let me give you as my last lesson for you in this course, inspired by Lincoln and his example at Gettysburg: Create empathy between yourself and your listeners; do it with your words. Combine ethos (the idea of personality) and pathos (the idea of healing) and shift the focus of your speech from "I" or "you" to "we". If we can remember to do that, we will have done one little step along the road that Lincoln wanted us to follow of being inspired by these men's lives to unite—in his thoughts as Americans, perhaps as us as human beings—but to act together to make sure that their sacrifices did indeed create a changed and a better world.

Along with the "Gettysburg Address," as I mentioned when we talked about Martin Luther King, Jr., up there on the walls of the Lincoln Memorial in Washington, DC are parts of the Second Inaugural Address, which has one of the most beautiful closes of any that I know. I'd like to use Lincoln's words as an inspiration for us as we continue to pursue his footsteps, he who has gone ahead of us in this world of public speaking, trying to measure up in some way to what his expectations would have been, to work at it as hard as he did. This is the end of his Second Inaugural Address, words for us to carry with us as we say farewell and go our separate ways: "With malice toward none, with charity for all, with firmness in the right as God gives us to see the right, let us strive on to finish the work we are in …"

Bibliography

Berkun, Scott. *Confessions of a Public Speaker*. New York: O'Reilly Media, 2009. A witty, insightful firsthand account of the life of a professional public speaker. Covers the more mundane, practical issues involved with public speaking while providing lively anecdotes and sound advice.

Blaisdell, Bob, ed. *Great Speeches by Native Americans.* New York: Dover Publications, 2000. Includes Tecumseh's speech, as well as other lesser-known addresses by Native Americans.

Carnegie, Dale. *The Art of Public Speaking.* New York: Cosimo Classics, 2007. The latest edition of the classic text in modern public speaking, written by a pioneer in social relations and personal development.

Dowis, Richard. *The Lost Art of the Great Speech: How to Write One—and How to Deliver It.* New York: AMA Publications, 2000. A step-by-step guide to crafting a great speech, from general organization to word choice to fielding questions from the audience. Includes excerpts from powerful historical speeches.

Safire, William. *Lend Me Your Ears: Great Speeches in History.* New York: W. W. Norton, 2007. An impressive compendium of great speeches, collected by a former presidential speechwriter and master of language. Includes the full texts of many of the speeches found in this course.

Credits

Steven K. Gragert and M. Jane Johansson, eds., *The Papers of Will Rogers: From the Broadway Stage to the National Stage*, Volume 3, September 1915–July 1928 (Norman: University of Oklahoma Press, 2005), pp. 364–366. Permission granted by Will Rogers Memorial Museums.

Notes

Notes

Notes

Notes

Notes

Notes